W9-CED-170

Reading for Life
The Learner as a Reader

Reading
for Life

The Learner as a Reader

Learning Media

First published 1996 for the New Zealand Ministry of Education
By Learning Media Limited under the title *The Learner as a Reader*
Copyright © Crown New Zealand 1996

This revised edition published 1997 by Learning Media Limited,
Box 3293, Wellington 6001, New Zealand
Web site: www.learningmedia.com
Copyright © Learning Media Limited 1997
All rights reserved. Inquires should be made to the publisher.

Distributed in the United States of America by
Pacific Learning, P.O. Box 2723,
Huntington Beach, CA 92647-0723
Web site: www.pacificlearning.com

10 9 8 7

Printed in Hong Kong

ISBN 0 478 20554 6

PL-9925

Contents

Introduction

Beliefs About Literacy Learning and Teaching That Underlie This Book

- Reading and writing experiences should be student-centered.

- Reading and writing for meaning are paramount.

- Writing and reading are inseparable processes.

- Literacy learning must be worthwhile.

- Children learn to read and write by reading and writing a wide variety of texts.

- Reading and writing are powerful tools for learning.

- The best approach to teaching reading and writing is a combination of approaches.

- Careful assessment of students' literacy learning is integral to sound teaching.

- Good first teaching is necessary for successful literacy learning.

- Reading and writing flourish in a supportive environment.

About This Book

Reading for Life is intended to help all teachers of students in the elementary grades improve their understanding of how children learn to read. It will also be of assistance to teachers of older students.

Reading for Life emphasizes the importance of reading for meaning, the importance of assessment and evaluation for good teaching, the requirement for critical reading of both literary and expository texts, the reader's need to integrate various sources of information, and the need for teachers to have good class management.

People write in order to record or communicate meaning, and they read to reconstruct and respond to that meaning. This book puts forward an interactive model of reading. Learning to read is an amazingly complex business. It involves integrating the learner's experience of life with the skills and strategies they have learned and with their knowledge of language, including syntax, spelling patterns, and phonological translations. The end product of this process, and the means to it, is meaning.

Like *Dancing with the Pen* (Wellington: Learning Media, 1992), this book recognizes the close relationship between reading and writing. Students learn a great deal about reading as they write, and about writing as they read. Literacy involves both reading and writing.

A book like this comes about only as the result of input and commitment from many different sources. Particular mention is due to the following.

The New Zealand Ministry of Education funded the first edition of this book for distribution to all New Zealand schools, thus keeping up a long tradition of providing to schools quality materials that underpin sound literacy education.

Ro Griffiths, respected literacy consultant in both New Zealand and the United States of America, helped to develop the vision for this book and has been a leader and guide throughout the project. Ro Griffiths developed this edition and brought new perspectives to the sections on the guided and shared reading approaches.

Lois Thompson, publishing manager for Learning Media, carried the vision forward by convening the writing and consultative teams who shaped and wrote this book. Lois Thompson brought to the project a depth of experience in literacy publishing, including the development of early reading series distributed internationally.

The team members with the major responsibility for writing the first edition were Margaret Hayes and Bas Stevenson, both widely known for their expertise as literacy consultants and teacher educators in New Zealand and the United States of America. Their knowledge of the learning of reading, soundly based in research, made a major contribution to the project. The other two writers in the team were Virginia Francis and Mary Hodgson, elementary school principals recognized for their leadership in classroom practice and in teacher education. Their practical wisdom ensured that the book would speak convincingly to teachers.

Sheena Hervey, literacy consultant and teacher educator with experience in both New Zealand and the United States, made valuable contributions which added to the quality of the text, particularly to the chapters on Knowing the Learner and Knowing the Approaches.

Peter Johnston, Professor of Education, The University of Albany, State University of New York, reviewed the text and brought valuable insights and new perspectives to the revision process, particularly to the section on assessment.

Acknowledgment is due finally to the many classroom teachers, teacher educators, consultants, and other literacy experts who contributed throughout the development and review process to ensure that this sound and authoritative text would result. Learning Media is proud to be associated with this body of expertise and to be the publisher of *Reading for Life.*

1 The Power of Literacy

The Power of Literacy

Reading opens up our understanding of many worlds — exciting, interesting, delightful, disturbing, factual, or fantastic. Through reading, we can find out when the next train goes or travel to the stars. Reading gives us the power to understand what others have written, today or thousands of years ago. It has the potential to change our lives.

We read for a variety of esthetic and academic purposes: for enjoyment and relaxation; to get information; to develop a skill; to follow directions; to find our way about; and to help develop an understanding of ourselves and of the world. Margaret Mahy believes that stories, read and told, help children to construct and find meaning in their lives. Like many children, she was read fairy tales and told many stories that were "invented from moment to moment … I readily used the characters and structures of these stories to discuss my own life."[1]

Literacy learning operates in a dynamic, evolving, social, and historical context that is constructed by individuals and groups as part of their everyday life. Social activities such as buying groceries, filling in an insurance form, writing to the editor, reading a bedtime story, taking part in a committee meeting, or surfing the Internet all contribute to literacy. Texts may be shared by communities of readers and writers for a wide range of purposes. They are often important for interaction in social situations, for example, within the family, at church, at clubs and organizations, and at the workplace.

Literacy is essential for living in society.

---

1   In a personal letter, 1995

Because it has so many different contexts, literacy involves reading and writing texts that use a variety of linguistic and symbolic codes. There are also different media. The television or computer screen is providing an increasingly significant medium for communication, and children are growing up familiar with these. New and changing technology in no way reduces society's demands for literacy; on the contrary, it increases them.

Literacy is not limited to paper and books.

> *The so-called electronic superhighway places even greater importance on literacy. Books may change in form, but the written word will remain the foundation of an ever more complex world, where the ability to source, interpret, and act on information will be critical. Excellent books will continue to inspire children, to drive their imagination and lift their creativity, and in so doing, shape our future.[2]*

Literacy is of central importance to learning in all curriculum areas. Effective literacy programs will emphasize the joy of reading and also focus on the need to expose students to a wide range of texts. (Some texts will be presented in print, while others will be conveyed through electronic or pictorial means.) The teacher's role is to provide all students with the opportunities and support they need to develop as keen, confident, and competent readers.

Language development is essential to intellectual growth. It enables us to make sense of the world around us.
The New Zealand Curriculum Framework, page 10

Making Sense of Experience

Most children learn to use language in an apparently easy and natural way. As babies, they are immersed in a sea of oral language. They hear the people they know talking to each other, talking about them, and talking to them. They hear talk on the radio, on television, in the street, at the shops. From what they hear, they work out what oral language is for and actively begin to construct a language to communicate their own ideas.

A baby's world is full of written language. Written words crowd in on every side — from the lettered cartons holding their toys, from television advertisements, calendars on the wall, magazines and books in the home, junk

mail in the letterbox, print on the computer screen, bright rows of cans and packets on the supermarket shelf, and the flashing lights of neon signs.

The knowledge required for children to learn to read and write comes from their experiences of talking and learning about the world and talking and learning about written language.

---

2 Murray Papps (National Manager, Lever Rexona NZ), in a speech at the 1995 Aim Book Awards

Reading Aloud and Storytelling

Adults have a vital role in helping children make sense of the world. Reading to children is one of the best ways of doing this. Dorothy Butler says:

> *It is my belief that there is no "parent's aid" which can compare with the book in its capacity to establish and maintain a relationship with a child. Its effects extend far beyond the covers of the actual book and invade every aspect of life.*[3]

Reading aloud to young children is very enjoyable for both reader and child. The stories and other texts help the children to bring order to their experience and, as they are read to, they build positive attitudes to books, attitudes that are likely to lead to future competence in reading. These benefits are greatest when the child has participated actively in the process of "being read to", talking and asking questions about the story and learning about letters and sounds, words and meanings.

Many excellent collections of stories, poems, and rhymes are available on audiotape with readalong texts and on interactive CD-ROM. Although the live, person-to-person experience is best of all, this kind of "reading aloud" is also valuable for children.

Storytelling includes both children's retelling of past or imagined events, and stories told or read to them by an adult or an older child. Storytelling is of paramount importance, not only because it helps in learning to read but also because the story form fosters intellectual, emotional, and spiritual growth.

> *It is almost certainly in childhood that children are most susceptible, both to living examples and to the examples they find in books. As children listen to stories, as they take down the books from library shelves, they may, as Graham Greene suggests in* The Lost Childhood, *be choosing their future and the values that will dominate it.*[4]

As stories are read and told to them again and again, children begin to get a feeling for what a story is and how stories in their own culture are structured — what kinds of beginnings, middles, and endings they have. Some children have listened to adults telling each other stories. Some have heard Bible stories and parables. Others have been brought up on picture books, legends, and fairy tales. What children think of as "a story" when they arrive at school varies from child to child.

Children need to be exposed to all kinds of written language, including reports, stories, diaries, speeches, poetry, directions, and persuasive writing. Teachers should help students at all levels to feel at home with the different forms (genres) that written language can take. Failure to do this denies the students part of their language heritage. It also denies them access to a medium that is critical for other kinds of learning.

---

3   D. Butler, *Babies Need Books,* 3rd ed. (London: Penguin, 1995), Introduction, p. xii
4   The Plowden Report, 1967 (section 595), quoted in H. M. Saxby, *Give Them Wings: The experience of children's literature* (Melbourne: Macmillan, 1987), p. 5

Learning How to Learn

From the very start, children are learning how to learn. They respond to their environment and to the reactions of others; they judge the effectiveness of what they have learned to do. Our relationship with the world is active from the beginning. "We grapple with it," says Margaret Donaldson, "we construe it intellectually, we represent it to ourselves." In so doing, we create our own model of the world, which we need "to help us to anticipate events and be ready to deal with them."[5]

Our model (the way we think the world operates) is constructed in our minds — we build our own private frame of reference. Later, when we learn to read, we bring this frame of reference to the printed page in an interaction between what we already know and what we are finding out.

Making sense of experience is a continuous process. It is also recursive, building on what has gone before. We visit a familiar experience again and again, bringing some new knowledge with us each time. Many happenings confirm and develop each individual's theory of the world. When new events don't fall easily into place, the old theory is reworked to accommodate new insights.

Learning is continuous and recursive.

Although such leaps ahead reward successful learners with new power, they do not occur without effort. Learners have to pause, reflect, and strive to develop new intellectual tools when they encounter language that does not immediately blend with their experience and their perception of reality. Information from several sources must be integrated, using whatever skills there are to hand. "From such brief tussles in moments of not quite understanding, the child learns more about language," says Marie Clay.[6]

Exploring Language and Thinking Critically

The social function of language is extremely important. Through conversation with peers and adults, a child's language is brought to higher and higher levels.

But we do not always talk things over with others. We often use language to find out what we think. Thinking includes thinking about language itself.

An important understanding about language occurs when a child begins to speculate about the nature of words. Children realize that words and the things words stand for are separate, that language can be talked about as well as talked with. They grasp, although not at first in a conscious, analytic way, that language is a symbolic system. Our language system, which stems from our social and cultural origins, represents reality to us and largely defines our thinking.

Conscious control over language comes from an understanding of how language works and from being able to

---

5   M. Donaldson, *Children's Minds* (London: Croom Helm Ltd, 1978), p. 68
6   M. M. Clay, *Becoming Literate: The construction of inner control* (Auckland: Heinemann, 1991), p. 73

describe, discuss, and analyze one's own language and the language of others. If students are to learn to talk about language, they need first to hear teachers using appropriate terms in the context of reading and writing texts. They will then be able to discuss language, meanings, and ideas in a range of texts, relating their understanding to experience, purpose, audience, and other texts.

Language is fundamental to thinking and learning.

Meeting the Learning Needs of Students

Teachers acknowledge that each child comes to school with at least five years of accumulated experience and that this experience should be valued and affirmed. The teacher's role is to start teaching from where the child is, to widen the range of the child's understandings, and to extend the child's knowledge.

Children learning to read and write become aware of language features in their own language.

Teachers need to provide students with "scaffolding." This means temporary support: teaching students in such a way that what they can do with help today, they can do by themselves tomorrow. Building on the literacy skills the students have and helping them know what they need to learn next, the teacher can give the students just the right amount of support and guidance.

For students who come from language backgrounds other than English, it is particularly important that the school recognizes and uses the language skills they already have. Such students need extra support to use their existing language competencies to understand and use English.

All teachers should affirm learners' home language and previous experiences.

In planning their language programs, teachers should consider each student's needs, learning styles, and present knowledge. If the teacher presents all students with the same specific task, the task will probably not be related to the needs of all. For each student, there is an area that is their current frontier of learning; an area where they cannot yet work independently but where they can learn to work with appropriate help from their teacher. This area is called the "zone of proximal development."[7] The teacher works with the student in that zone, by using scaffolding.

Literacy programs should be learner-centered.

The Conditions for Learning

Smith (1978), Holdaway (1979), and Cambourne (1988) have described the conditions under which young children learn to use oral language and develop emergent literacy behaviors. They argue that these conditions should be duplicated as far as possible in the classroom to assist successful literacy development. The version of these conditions that follows is modeled after Cambourne (1988).[8] Cambourne says that, for a child to learn effectively, there must be immersion, demonstrations, engagement, expectations, responsibility, approximations, use, and response. These conditions are vitally important in reading classes at all levels, not just in the early years.

---

7 L. S. Vygotsky, *Mind in Society* (Cambridge, Massachusetts: Harvard University Press, 1978)
8 B. Cambourne, *The Whole Story: Natural learning and the acquisition of literacy in the classroom.* (Auckland: Ashton Scholastic Limited, 1988). Another description of the enabling conditions may be found in *Dancing with the Pen* (Wellington: Learning Media, 1992), pp. 11–20

Literacy development requires interaction with the text and active participation by the reader.

Immersion

Just as babies need a supportive community of speakers when they are learning to talk, students need to be surrounded by written texts, at home and at school, when they are learning to read and write.

They need a classroom environment that is alive with books and reading matter of all kinds, where their own writing is displayed and shared, and where there is ready access to computers and data sources. Reading aloud to students should take place almost every day. Writing and shared, guided, and independent reading should be everyday activities.

Demonstrations

To become aware of different kinds of text, students need to see demonstrations of people reading and writing different kinds of text. Teachers and other students can model such things as how to find information, how to write paragraphs, how to find the main points in an article, how to recognize certain literary or grammatical features in a text, how to recognize the rhyming words in a poem, or how to spell a word. Demonstrations need to be repeated in different ways and in different contexts because students will not grasp all the information when it is first presented and different students learn in different ways. When demonstrating, teachers can talk out loud about what they are doing and why as they model it.

Engagement

Immersion and demonstrations are not sufficient on their own. For learning to be effective, students need to engage actively with the language in which they are immersed and with the activities and strategies they see demonstrated. Active learners take over ideas, skills, and knowledge as they observe demonstrations of reading — they appropriate what they have seen and make something of it for themselves.

For this act of ownership to take place, learners need to see themselves as potential readers; they need to see the reading as desirable for them; and they need to be successful. Then they will be confident — eager to get into gear, to engage, and to move forward — and will not be put off by a false start or two.

Expectations and Praise

Expectation, value, and praise are key factors in encouraging success. The confidence that others show in students is the most powerful aid to their learning.

Success is necessary for all of us — we don't care to fall down too often. However, learners are not hindered by the fear of failure when others convey to them, with matter-of-fact assurance, that they will succeed and that the mistakes made along the way are stepping-stones to that success. Firm support, and warm praise when they solve a current problem, will see them through the parts they find most difficult.

Positive expectations of students, and praise for the efforts they make, are key factors leading to success in reading.

Responsibility

When they first come to school, most students need to share with their teacher the responsibility for learning to read. As they are given increasing responsibility for their own learning, they begin to work out problems for themselves and to choose learning activities that are particularly relevant to their needs. For example, students gradually learn to select their own material when searching for information from the library or when reading independently. In work across the curriculum, it is especially important that learners are encouraged to question for themselves and are given the responsibility for finding their own answers.

Approximations and Risks

All learning involves taking risks, and risk taking is essential for people learning to read. Learners will be willing to risk making their own approximations when their experience shows that their attempts are accepted. Initially, the teacher's responses should focus on the meaning of what is read rather than on inaccuracies of form or detail.

By accepting their approximations and asking questions that will help them make meaning from the text, the teacher can help students learn to use appropriate strategies so that, eventually, they will gain the skill and confidence to regulate their own reading.

Teachers need to encourage students to take risks, and should accept their approximations as they learn to read.

Practice and Use

There is plenty of evidence to show that the more exposure to texts students have, the better readers they are likely to become. Stanovich (1992) describes a study where there was a twenty-fold difference in the number of words encountered weekly between the best and least able readers in year three and year five children. He goes on to say that,

> *Lack of exposure and practice on the part of the less-skilled reader delays the development of automaticity and speed at the word recognition level. Slow, capacity-draining word recognition processes require cognitive resources that should be allocated to higher-level processes of text integration and comprehension. Thus, reading for meaning is hindered, unrewarding reading experiences multiply, and practice is avoided or merely tolerated without real cognitive involvement.[9]*

Language and knowledge about language develop principally through using language.

Expert readers are people who have developed a large repertoire of skills and understandings related to reading and language. Such skills come only with practice.

Practice should occur in the course of purposeful reading. It should not be imposed in the form of trivial tests, repetitive exercises, or meaningless drills. Such activities can hinder the development of real language skills. Genuine reading practice echoes the way in which children practice learning to talk or walk or ride a bike. Because they want so much to acquire that skill, there is no limit to the time and trouble they will take to master it — it isn't work, it is life.

Response

All parents expect their children to learn to talk. They accept with enthusiasm each child's attempts to communicate, attending to the message rather than requiring strict grammatical correctness. This approach provides a good model for teachers of reading.

Response is feedback — it involves one human being reacting to another, and it is important that feedback be honest as well as positive. The teacher needs to offer genuine responses and to communicate with students about the texts that they are actually reading. Praise or encouragement need not always be expressed in words — facial expressions and other body language may be even more convincing. Children, like adults, are keenly aware of the nuances of body language, and some are particularly sensitive. Although students come from different cultures and social groups, practically all of them will react with a glow of pride and pleasure to genuine interest and honest, positive feedback.

Responses must be informed, genuine, and encouraging.

---

9   K. E. Stanovich, *Differences in Reading Acquisition: Causes and consequences,* paper presented at the Eighteenth New Zealand Conference on Reading, Wellington, May 1992 (Ontario Institute for Studies in Education), pp. 4–5

Language and Cultural Difference

In every society, there are many different cultures. This means that students learn in different ways, and some may find the rules for using language in the classroom different from those they have learned at home. Children from different social groups, too, grow up experiencing different forms of language and social interaction. The forms and characteristic patterns of the language they learn first affect the ways in which students communicate with others, both at home and at school. Their spoken and written language reflects the social environment in which they grow.[10] Demanding that students change this language for that of a different cultural pattern may have the effect of distancing them from their family. It may cut at the heart of who they are.

Language development is based on the language that learners already have and is inextricably linked with their gender, social and cultural backgrounds, and individual needs.
English in the New Zealand Curriculum, page 13

If teachers are to help students develop their private and home language patterns to meet the needs of a wider world, they will have to offer help in ways that are tactful and respectful. They must find ways, because schools are responsible for empowering students through effective language programs. For example, teachers can lead students to realize that different forms of language are appropriate for different contexts and occasions. They can help them to become articulate in standard and public uses of the English language. Schools also need to expose students to the patterns of cultures that are different from their own.

Teaching approaches should reflect students' diverse cultural backgrounds.

It is important not to impose stereotypes on students' language abilities. Some children come from families where literacy is valued. Others who do not have this experience may have come from a family with rich oral resources. The role of the teacher is to be aware of these differences, to be sensitive to them, and to build on the competencies each student brings to the classroom.

It has been found (for example, by Cazden[11] and McNaughton[12]) that classrooms with organized and focused activities for peer learning are beneficial to students whose first language is not English.

---

10 S. McNaughton et al. "A Literacy Environment is not Separable from the Ecology, the Social Fabric, of the Family," *Two Studies of Transitions: Socializations of Literacy, and Te Hiranga Taketake: Mai i te kohanga reo ki te kura* (Research Unit for Māori Education, Department of Education, University of Auckland, 1990), p. 55

11 C. Cazden, *Classroom Discourse: The language of teaching and learning* (Portsmouth, New Hampshire: Heinemann, 1988)

12 S. McNaughton, *Being Skilled: The socializations of learning to read* (London: Methuen, 1987)

Children need a firm base in their own language and culture.

It is now well known that children need to develop a secure base in their own world before they are immersed in the language and culture of the school. Preferably, they need a firm base both in their culture and in the language of their culture. Children who do not get this base often miss out both at home and at school.

Teachers need to be aware that their own value systems can influence their expectations.

Teachers should take care that their own value systems do not influence their expectations of what students can achieve. Courtney Cazden's interesting analysis of classroom discourse shows how teachers' unfamiliarity with the language patterns of the students they teach can affect the way they correct reading "errors."[13] David Wood says this about teachers' expectations:

> *Teachers … perceive children who do not talk using "received pronunciation" and the 'standard' form of their language as less able or less well motivated than children whose talk corresponds more closely to that of the currently 'dominant' dialect. Making (perhaps implicit or unconscious) judgments about children's educational potential on the basis of how they talk, teachers set up self-fulfilling prophecies which lead to the anticipated differences in levels of achievement. Crudely, because teachers expect less of children from some social backgrounds, these children are taught and learn less.*[14]

13 Cazden, *Classroom Discourse: The language of teaching and learning*, pp. 81–4
14 D. Wood, *How Children Think and Learn* (New York: Basil Blackwell, 1988), p. 112

Further advice about social differences and how these relate to oral and written language may be found in the work of Shirley Brice Heath.[15]

By seeking opportunities to build on the social interaction and language patterns of the student's home culture, a teacher can often allay fears and avoid misunderstandings. The language of their own social group and ethnic background can work for students at school rather than against them. Co-operation between parents and teachers is of enormous benefit in bridging the gaps.

---

15 S. B. Heath, *Ways with Words: Language, life and work in communities and classrooms* (Cambridge: Cambridge University Press, 1983)

2 The Reading Process

How Do We Read?

Try to think what you're doing as you read the following texts.

> The Chrysler Building is a famous New York landmark. Once the tallest building in the world (until the opening of the Empire State Building a year later), it was also one of the first buildings to feature exposed metal in its design. The building was designed by William Van Allen and opened in 1930.

> You can switch a color from "Spot" to "Process" (or vice versa). However you may need to adjust the resulting color values (using a printed swatch book as a reference) for a converted process color to print as you expect. If, for example, you convert a spot color with RGB values to a process color with CMYK values, the resulting color only approximates the original color. (If you specified CMYK values for a spot color, PageMaker retains those values when you convert the color.)[16]

What is each of these texts about?

Did you meet any difficulties when reading these texts?

If so, what were they? How did you overcome them?

Did you read every word?

Did you anticipate any words or predict what the text was about?

Did you immediately recognize the meaning of every word?

Did you reread any sections or spend longer on some words than others?

How important were your past experiences in helping you understand the texts?

Fluent reading is the product of a complex combination of knowledge, skills, and understandings. All readers, from the beginning reader to the fluent adult reader, have to use and integrate various kinds of information to create meaning from text.

Readers need to expect that text will make sense. The reading process can be described as creating meaning from text by making connections between what is read and what is already known. Skilled readers at all stages work this way. They bring vital information to any act of reading and use this information to interact with the print information in the text.

We also make judgments as we read. The ability to respond critically to what is significant in a text develops as readers gain experience of life and of a

Reading for meaning involves the reader in working with information from a variety of sources.

---

16 *Aldus PageMaker User Manual* (Aldus Corporation, USA, 1993), p. 155

wide variety of texts. Students' sophistication in critical response grows, gradually, from the earliest stages of reading acquisition. Teachers can foster this growth by giving their students guidance and plenty of opportunities to respond and to think critically about a range of texts.

Prior Knowledge — Bringing Information to Text

Skilled readers don't just process information available from the print — they bring vital information to any act of reading. This information includes:

Reading is the interaction between sources of information in the text and the reader's prior knowledge.

- general knowledge about the world;

- visual information from the text;

- phonological information from the reader's experience of oral language;

- knowledge of the relationships between letters and sounds;

- knowledge about how written and oral language relate;

- knowledge of the way language is structured;

- knowledge about how texts are organized.

Comprehension is not reached in a single act; it is a constant and recurring process of accommodation and adjustment. We build understanding by engaging in a series of recursive interactions between what is in our head and what is on the page or screen. The understanding we gain from text probably resembles the author's original meaning, but no reader rebuilds exactly the same meaning as the author, nor do any two readers' perceptions of the meaning of a text coincide precisely. Each of us prints our own personal stamp on every act of reading we undertake.

Sources of Information

The information used by a reader to construct meaning can be discussed under three major categories: meaning or semantic cues, structural or syntactic cues, and visual cues including phonological awareness.

Meaning Cues

Semantic information is associated with meaning — with the ideas presented in the text and in any pictures and diagrams. The meaning a reader finds in the text, however, will always depend on what the reader brings to the text. Meanings differ according to experience. If you live in the United States of America, "freezing workers" are any workers who are very cold. In New Zealand, they are employees in the meat industry. The question for a reader is: "Does it make sense?" If it doesn't, then the reader has to do more work, adding to the sum total of their experiences, until it does.

Structural Cues

Knowing the syntax and grammatical structure of a language enables the reader to anticipate the correct parts of speech, or the order of words in a sentence, while reading. As experienced readers of English, we can tell that the word spelled "read" is different in the following two sentences because of where it occurs in the sentence.

> Matthew likes to read.   He has read the book.

Here the important question for the reader is: "Can this word be said this way in this place in the sentence?" If it can't, then the reader has to look for another solution to the problem.

Visual Cues and Phonological Information

Visual cues include graphic information, such as the printed letters on the page, and the conventions of print, such as spacing and direction. These enable the reader to identify sentences, groups of words, whole words, individual letters, or patterns of letters in clusters, affixes, and roots. The key question for the reader is: "Does it look right?"

Print conventions include directional principles (for example, reading from left to right, line after line, on the page), the use of spaces, capital and lower case letters, and punctuation. Many of these conventions indicate where a sentence, a word, or a paragraph begins and ends. They can also show what part of speech a word is, in a particular sentence. For example, compare "At the picnic we had ham sandwiches, fruit salad, and lemonade," with "At the picnic we had ham, sandwiches, fruit, salad, and lemonade."

Phonics — the relationship between oral language and graphic symbols or the relationships between letters and sounds — is also a crucial source of

Visual cues and phonological information overlap because the spelling patterns that are part of phonological information are also visual.

Learning to use the correspondences between words and their sounds (phonics) is a necessary part of learning to read.

Reading and writing experiences further develop phonological awareness.

information for readers. This kind of information is partly visual, partly aural, and partly memory. The letter-sound relationships identified may be between single letters and sounds, clusters of letters and sounds, or whole words.

A learner's understanding of the sound sequences in spoken words is called phonological awareness. With practice in hearing the sounds within words, children can learn letter-to-sound or sound-to-letter relationships.

At a very simple level, phonological awareness develops as children discriminate sounds in rhymes. At a more advanced level, children segment sounds in words and use that knowledge to form new words. At a later level still, children focus on spelling-to-sound correspondences.

Children develop phonological awareness by being read to, by reading for themselves, by discussions about words, by reading rhymes, jingles, and poems aloud, and by writing, as they attempt to spell words they want to write. They gradually learn to appreciate phonological aspects of language such as rhyme, alliteration, and assonance. Phonological awareness involves the ability to manipulate, or play with, sound segments in words. (Refer to page 42 for more information about phonological awareness.)

Integrating the Sources of Information

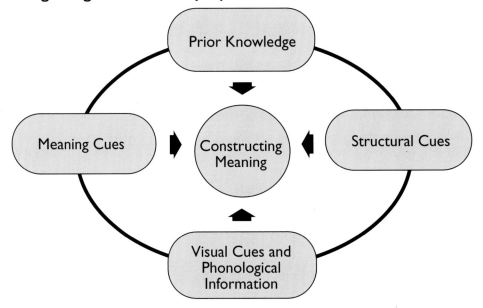

A reader brings meaning to the text from many sources. When a reader learns to integrate these sources, the creation of meaning becomes almost instantaneous except when the text is particularly challenging.

The following example of a running record shows a student using meaning cues, structural cues, and some visual cues to produce a verb at "woke up"; visual cues and phonological information at "felt"; and print conventions to return to the beginning of the second sentence because the meaning has been lost.

SC means "self-corrects." The arrow indicates the point to which the student returned in rereading the text — R means rereads. In this running record, the teacher's observations of the student reading were originally recorded on a blank piece of paper; the text that was read has been added here for the sake of clarity. Refer to pages 56–63 for more about running records.

Strategies for Processing Text Information

In this book, the word "strategies" refers to the various ways a reader uses information or searches for cues in a text to construct meaning. Attending, searching, anticipating, checking, confirming, and self-correcting are the strategies through which that process takes place. For experienced readers, the process seems to be largely automatic.

In discussing reading with the writers of this book, Marie Clay has described strategies as the cognitive and perceptual activities initiated by the child to get to the message of the text.

Readers' Strategies

Attend and Search	where the reader focuses on the text and looks for specific information
Anticipate	where the reader forms expectations about the print, based on prior knowledge and information from the text
Check	where the reader checks that the chosen response makes sense and matches information already processed
Confirm	where the reader accepts the response
Self-correct	where the reader notices a mismatch, tries again, and produces an accurate response

The Emergent, Early, and Fluent Stages of Reading

For the purposes of this book, reading development is divided into three broad, overlapping stages: emergent, early, and fluent.

The Emergent Stage

At this stage, readers are making a start. They are learning that a book has a special way of telling a story that allows readers to go back to it as often as they like, that the words stay the same, that the pictures create their own meaning and help readers to understand the story, that the story has a shape and the author a voice. They are learning to expect to make sense of what is read to them and what they read. They are beginning to understand that certain information exists in text and are finding out how to access it. These characteristics of emergent readers demonstrate that students are beginning to use semantic, syntactic, visual, and phonological information to gain meaning.

The Early Stage

Readers at the early stage will expect to get meaning from the text. This is when learning readers establish the attitudes and understandings of reading for meaning as they become increasingly skillful at using visual and phonological information. Early readers learn more about reading strategies each time they read. They begin to integrate their use of the sources of information — meaning, structure, visual cues, and phonics — as they continue to attend, search, anticipate, and self-correct. Students are moving towards integrating reading processes with ease.

The Fluent Stage

At this stage, readers are able to create meaning from longer and more complex texts. They are learning to adjust the way they read to overcome the challenges they meet in the specialized styles, forms, and vocabularies of different kinds of text. They are reading fluently, gaining direct access to information in text through immediate visual recognition of familiar vocabulary. They need not give as much of their attention to the actual print as they did at the early stage. As they create meaning from a variety of texts, fluent readers evaluate the usefulness and significance of the texts against their purpose for reading.

The characteristics of fluent readers demonstrate that students are beginning to adapt reading processes and strategies for different purposes. In this book, we occasionally refer to older fluent readers, to distinguish these from children who become fluent readers at quite a young age.

A student's stage of development across the range of text types will not necessarily be uniform. A student may show most of the characteristics of fluent readers when reading a particular type of text. On another type of text, as adjustments are made to a new style or form or to a different level of challenge, the student's reading processing may slow down.

For a more detailed description of the attitudes, understandings, and behaviors of emergent, early, and fluent readers, see pages 50–53.

The stages of reading are not necessarily transferable across the range of text types.

Problem Solving and the Fluent Reader

In the emergent and early stages of reading development, the teacher can hear and observe the reader's use of strategies. With fluent readers, the process of reading becomes a silent one as they visually analyze print (quickly recognizing most relevant features and using phonological information), make links with what they already know, and integrate meaning and structural sources of information. Fluent readers are required to make more inferences and bring more background to the reading than is necessary at the emergent and early stages.

For example, when a fluent reader is reading text at an appropriate level of support and challenge, the reader's immediate responses to the text may not be observable when the student is reading orally. The problem-solving strategies of attending and searching, anticipating, checking, confirming, and self-correcting are all likely to be occurring in the reader's head. However, all teachers need to be aware of these problem-solving strategies so that they can help students at all stages of development to use them when necessary.

It is the ability to use reading strategies quickly, confidently, and with ever-increasing independence that activates what Marie Clay calls a reader's "self-extending system," a response system that extends its own capacity.

When students use strategies successfully and independently, they activate their own self-extending system.

Early instruction in the use of strategies helps students to learn how to learn, as they actively solve problems that relate to the challenges they meet in new text and as they find ways of overcoming these challenges for themselves. Teachers who help students in this sort of way are providing scaffolding for them (refer to page 13).

The following example shows a student who is developing a self-extending system and overcoming challenge in text for herself.

He went back to the house

where the goats lived

child: That's 'lived' isn't it?
Teacher: What do you think?
child: It is.
Teacher: How do you know?
child: It's got a different ending.

Children who feel that their own experiences and contributions to learning are accepted and valued will have a secure base from which to transfer the skills and understandings they are learning, using them to solve new problems and try new ways of working.

Understandings about Reading

Through gaining messages from reading and composing messages in writing, the reader gradually acquires some important understandings about text and the reading process.

Understandings about Text

- Written texts, like spoken language, have the power to delight or dismay, to enlighten or confuse, to challenge, to inform, to excite, and to satisfy.

- Written texts, like spoken language, will almost certainly make sense.

- Texts do not contain one finite meaning that will be "unlocked" by all readers. The meaning that a reader creates from a text will be based on their prior knowledge.

- Texts provide the answers to many questions and help people to understand themselves and the world.

- The conventions of print are consistent.

- Texts of different genres are structured in different ways. Knowing how different genres work makes them easier to comprehend.

Understandings about the Reading Process

- The meaning of a text is created by integrating information from various sources.

- A reader may attend to clusters of letters or recognize familiar words directly.

- Risk taking is essential for efficient reading.

- Self-extension in reading is achieved by using a network of strategies flexibly and independently.

The Link between the Processes of Reading and Writing

Marie Clay points out that:

For children who learn to write at the same time as they learn to read, writing plays a significant part in the early reading progress.[17]

This is because there is a reciprocal relationship between reading and writing (see *Dancing with the Pen*, Wellington: Learning Media, 1993, page 10). Both reading and writing are concerned with the communication of meaning, and each process has its own special characteristics. The reader interacts with the symbols on the page to recreate meaning (ideas). The writer starts with ideas and has to represent these with symbols, using an appropriate literary style to suit the intended audience. Writers create meaning using the same conventions of print that readers encounter when reading existing texts. A student who has worked hard to establish meaning in a personal piece of writing is well equipped to search for meaning in the writings of others. Reading goes hand in hand with writing, and teachers should make this link clear to learners.

> Reading goes hand in hand with writing, and teachers should make this link clear to learners.

Complementary Skills and Understandings

Many complementary skills and understandings are gained through reading and writing. As they read and write, students confirm that:

- written text, like speech, is a source of interest and enjoyment;

- writing fixes and clarifies personal experience, just as reading enables entry into the experiences of others;

- their written text makes sense because, in producing their own writing, they have had to put their ideas into a form that will make sense for others;

- relationships of meaning exist between new words and words already known;

- there are different styles of language, and the styles used in writing often differ from the styles of spoken language.

The reading process involves two main tasks that are complementary: visual analysis of print, and understanding of text. Don Holdaway emphasizes that it is not appropriate to assume that one of these activities precedes the other and should be taught first. The two activities are interdependent. "Reading" words without understanding is "a string of meaningless noise." Understanding a text without having processed it is impossible, "an empty dream — a figment of the imagination. Neither is reading: reading is both."[18]

> Visual analysis of text and comprehending text are complementary tasks.

---

17 M. M. Clay, *What Did I Write?* (Auckland: Heinemann, 1973), p. 70
18 D. Holdaway, *Independence in Reading: A handbook on individualized procedures* (Auckland: Ashton Educational, 1972), pp. 21–2

3 Developing the Strategies of Beginning Readers

The Teacher's Role

Learning to read is a gradual process that requires the teacher to provide careful direction, monitoring, and support. The support offered should be flexible and responsive. The student's need for support is temporary — it reduces over time as the learner becomes more willing and able to handle the responsibility of taking the next learning step.

In the first year of school, the role of the teacher is to provide opportunities for all children, no matter where they start from, to widen the range of their experiences and increase their understandings about talking and listening, reading and writing.

Through careful observation, the teacher can gather information about the student's attitudes to reading and current understandings and can work out what the student needs to learn next. Teachers should begin by noticing what children bring to reading and writing from the varied language experiences and cultural values of their home and community environments.

Teachers should not expect all children to display all the characteristics of an emergent reader within a set time. Some children will already be displaying some of them when they start school. Others will need several months of listening to different texts, taking part in shared reading and writing sessions, and learning about the alphabet and letter-sound relationships before such characteristics begin to appear.

Careful monitoring of students' reading behavior is essential.

Keeping Things in Context

Students learn to read best in a context where reading has meaning. They learn more about how to use the sources of information when teachers call attention to these in the course of real, purposeful reading and writing. For example, teachers can call attention to phonological and visual features in rhyming words (or in words that start the same way) when they are introducing and discussing texts with a group in the course of shared writing. They can highlight these features in combination with the sources of information that the student can already use.

Learning about the sources of information should occur in the course of authentic reading.

Teachers can also guide and encourage students to learn about the conventions of print in context, as they model writing and reading texts, and as the students read and write their own messages. A student focusing on print may, for example, temporarily isolate a letter and identify a word that begins with that letter. However, any learning of separate items is best combined with other sources of information. Items learned separately need to be "taken back into reading." This means that any item that has been isolated for attention is looked at again in its original context. It also means that what has been learned is later applied in other contexts.

Keeping Things Interesting

The essential attitudes, understandings, and strategies are learned best as students read texts that:

- have special meaning and interest for them;

- connect with their experience;

- use natural language;

- have an appropriate balance of supportive and challenging features;

- are enjoyable and appealing;

- expand readers' views of themselves and the world.

Attending and Searching

Emergent and early readers need to learn to attend to letters and words.

A student who notices a detail in a picture or a diagram is attending. A student who has learned the shape of the letter that begins her name can search a text to pick out that letter. The gradual development of these fledgling skills comes as students read and discuss many easy and familiar texts. Attending and searching skills include:

- using prior knowledge;

- anticipating the structure of the sentence or the next step in the story;

- using previous experiences with print (including analysis of sounds or clusters of sounds);

- using known words from reading and writing;

- using clusters of letters from known words to get to new words;

- using information from illustrations and diagrams.

For example, teachers can focus students' attention on particular letters and letter clusters as part of handwriting and spelling sessions. Or they can use techniques, such as a masking device, during shared reading, or a small teaching easel during shared or guided reading.

Anticipation

We rarely read a text without anticipating what will come next. This may be the next event in a story, the next word in a sentence, or the next step in an argument. Readers' anticipations about text are made on the basis of semantic, syntactic, visual, and phonological information. The skill of anticipating becomes both more precise and more all-encompassing as the student gains reading experience. For example, a reader seeing a picture of an empty nest anticipates that the story is about birds; or, when seeing the word "salsa," anticipates that the text may relate to something about food.

Syntactic, visual, and phonological sources of information are often used in combination. Readers know (though they may not be able to explain why) that some words have to be read or said in a particular way (for example, "several books" not "several book"), that certain letters regularly appear with others (for example, "th" and "ing"), and that some such clusters regularly appear in particular positions in words.

Anticipations about text are based on a variety of sources.

Building Anticipation — an Example

An introductory discussion of *Greedy Cat is Hungry*[19] for shared reading may involve a general discussion about cats and questions such as:

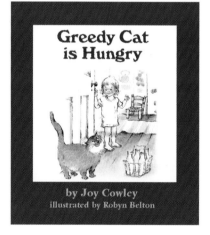

- *How do you know when your cat is hungry?*

- *So what does your cat do? So does my cat! And does your cat also sit by the fridge and meow?*

- *What does the title* Greedy Cat is Hungry *tell us about the story?*

- *Look at the picture on the cover. What is happening here?*

- *What is Greedy Cat doing?*

- *What is Katie doing?*

Ideas and words that are unfamiliar to any of the students should come up naturally in the course of this kind of discussion.

By building up students' experience and knowledge in ways like this, linking new ideas to known ones and discussing people's opinions, values, and feelings about the ideas, the teacher can deepen and refine students' background information so that they are better able to meet the ideas of the author.

Teachers need to build on the understandings students bring to reading.

---

19 J. Cowley, *Greedy Cat is Hungry*, Guided Reading series (Wellington: Learning Media Limited, 1997)

Using Anticipation in the Reading Session

Anticipation can be maintained during reading by asking questions such as:

- *I wonder what could happen now?*

- *Oh. I thought that might happen.*

- *Oh, no! I think on the next page we'll find that …*

Teachers should reinforce anticipations that show the student's use of specific prior knowledge.

It is important that teachers encourage students to use their prior knowledge to anticipate. This means praising responses even if the response was not successful in anticipating the text.

The following example shows a teacher working with a group of students who are developing an understanding of anticipation in reading. She uses an oral cloze process by stopping at key points in the narrative and leaving the students to fill in the gap. The text is *A Good Knee for a Cat* by Margaret Mahy, and the approach is shared reading.[20] Here, the teacher is using the pictures and her own actions to help the children understand how to anticipate.

Teacher	"The old cat got off his … " (mimes getting off her chair).
Children	Chair!
Teacher	"… and came over to Anna's wheelchair. He smelled its …" (points to picture).
Children	Wheels.
Teacher	"Then he jumped up on Anna's…" (pats her knee).
Children	Knee.

Texts that have lively repetitive structures and rhyme are ideal for helping children learn how to anticipate words.

Anticipation and the Language of Books

When books of all kinds are read to them, children become familiar with the various forms of written language. They begin to hear differences between what books say and what is said to them in everyday talk. These differences are in the choice of vocabulary, in word order and language structure, and in the patterning of sentences. Examples of book language are: "It is night"; "In a dark jungle lived a gorilla …"; "Off came our socks"; "But the crab wriggles and jiggles and falls."

---

20 M. Mahy, *A Good Knee for a Cat*, Guided Reading Series (Wellington: Learning Media Limited, 1997)

Children begin to make use of this knowledge to aid anticipation. When they hear, "Once upon a time …," they know that a story of a special kind is about to start. When they see a heading, "How to Make an Origami Frog," they expect a series of instructions to follow.

Confirmation and Self-correction

Creating meaning as we read and ensuring that what we read makes sense provides us with continuous feedback. To confirm information, we generally select further information from the available sources and cross-check. When reading, we monitor our own reading by searching text and cross-checking between several sources. This processing often turns a partially correct response into a correct one. A beginning reader may notice that there is a mismatch between what is read and what is in the picture, or that a word does not make sense in the sentence, or that there is a mismatch between what is read and what a word looks like. Knowing there is a problem is the first step. Knowing how to solve it is the next.

When "things are not quite right," students may be seen to:

- reread along a line of print from the beginning of the sentence;

- reread one or two words or make several attempts at the word;

- look uncertain or appeal for help, indicating that they have noticed a mismatch.

The following running record shows a student anticipating, searching, and rereading. This behavior leads to incorrect first responses being self-corrected.

Beginning readers need to understand the differences between oral language and book language.

Reading for meaning provides its own feedback.

35

The teacher can help students anticipate, confirm, and self-correct by ensuring that the students are:

- reading texts that are not too difficult in concepts and language or too far outside their experience;

- given time to work things out for themselves and that their attempts to self-monitor are reinforced;

- taking responsibility for confirming and correcting their anticipation by responding to questions such as, "Does that make sense?" or "Does that look right?" or "How do you know?";

- using their knowledge of the available sources of information and learning to combine these in various ways while they are reading for meaning.

Learning about Print Information

Most of the information on the page has to be processed by the reader.

Students' ability to implement the strategies using their knowledge of meaning and grammar is anchored in their oral language. However, from their earliest attempts at reading, they have to pay particular attention to print. In a program that emphasizes the use of books from the start, children begin to search with their eyes to find details that they can interpret. To ensure that this occurs, teachers draw attention to these details in the context of meaningful reading and writing.

Students usually (but not always) pay increasing attention to print details during the first year of school. As well as ensuring that students are reading for meaning, therefore, the teacher should check that they are actively learning about print information and the characteristics of written text. This is an essential part of learning to read.

There are three sources of print information that the student needs to know and work with when learning to read: concepts about print, visual information, and phonological patterns.

I.   *Concepts about Print*

It is important to monitor students' progress, to ensure that they are learning the essential concepts about print.

Concepts that children need to learn about print include directional movement, one-to-one matching (of spoken words to printed words), and book conventions.

Directional movement and one-to-one word matching are modeled by the teacher during shared reading and writing. One very effective way of highlighting concepts about print and particular print information is to use a pointer or a masking device with enlarged texts during shared reading. The masking card can be used to isolate words and letters, to help children understand particular terms, and to locate important punctuation marks or special positions (for example, the position of the first or last letter in a word or the first or last word in a sentence).

Guided reading provides further teaching opportunities. For example, teachers can demonstrate the skill of attending to print information by using a small teaching easel to draw attention to details of print in the text. A guided reading lesson gives teachers a chance to observe whether print conventions are being used by individual readers, as students take responsibility for reading the text for themselves. Concepts about print are reinforced strongly when students practice writing their own messages.

Skillful teaching is required to focus the student's attention on the details of print while ensuring that the message of the text and the enjoyment of the story are not lost.

Shared and guided reading provide effective opportunities to focus attention on print information.

2. *Visual Information*

Students need to acquire experience and knowledge of the visual sequences and shapes of print. These include the spelling patterns through which letters are formed into words, the patterns of words within longer units such as sentences and paragraphs, and the layout of text on the printed page.

Visual information includes:

- features of letters, for example, dots, tails, crossbars, or curves;

- differences in how letters are formed, for example, the distinction between the left- and right-hand facing of the upright to the circle in letters such as "d" and "b";

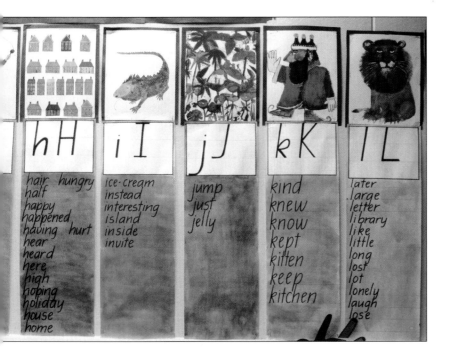

- characteristics of significant individual letters, for example, in the beginning letter of a student's name;

- clusters of letters, such as "thr" at the beginning of "thread" and "through," or "ook" in "book" and "look";

- the shape of individual words, for example, the length of the word "escalator," the height and shortness of the word "I," or the configuration of clusters such as "thr" and "ook";

- the various forms of particular printed letters such as g/g and a/ a, and different forms within one font, such as *italics* or **bold** type;

- the layout of text, for example, speech balloons within pictures, the positioning of captions underneath pictures, the carryover of text from one page to another, the length of the line, or the amount of text per page;

- the relationship of illustrations to text;

- the differences between pictures and symbols — for example, a STOP sign gives a message in a different way from a picture of a car stopping.

Learning the Letters of the Alphabet

Knowing the letters of the alphabet is important in early reading and writing.

Before they come to school, some children begin to "play" with writing in the same way that they "play" with reading, producing writing-like scribbles to carry their messages. They show interest in the print around them on signs, labels, and television; they enjoy alphabet songs and rhymes, and they learn to write their names. By the time they enter school, some children are likely to know the alphabet and recognize many upper- and lowercase letters. Where this is not so, teachers must help children learn these things, since recognizing letters is necessary for success in early reading and writing.

Children in the early stages of reading and writing may refer to different letters in a variety of ways. They may use letter names, or refer to a letter by a sound it stands for, or refer to it in an associated word — "That's the first letter in my name." It does not matter how children discriminate and identify letters as long as they do it. However, the teacher should generally use letter names when referring to letters. This is because letter names provide consistent labels for letter symbols and, in most cases, provide some clues for the sounds commonly associated with them.

The learning of letter names is most effective when it is enjoyable and its purpose is clear. Teachers should use letter names naturally in the course of reading and writing (and when children are learning handwriting), and they should make it clear to children that a knowledge of the alphabet is useful. Here are some ways to achieve this.

- Build up a large, clear, wall frieze of the alphabet, get the children to add examples to it regularly, and show them how to use it.

- Ensure that attractively illustrated alphabet books and simple dictionaries are available, and give guidance on their use.

- Get the children to make their own alphabet books individually, as a group or as a class, using children's own drawings or pictures cut out from magazines.

- Share texts and sing songs that use alphabet rhymes and games.

- Play alphabet games that link letter names with words (for example, I Spy).

- Use magnetic letters, colored paper cutouts of letters, sand tables, letters made with sandpaper or felt, and tracing paper.

- Provide a personal alphabet card for the child to use. Show them how it is used, and encourage them to use it when writing.

When children are learning about letters, the teacher should take examples from their reading and writing and help them notice the same letter in different contexts. For children, the difficult part of the task is not recognizing the letters in isolation but using their knowledge of the letters when they are reading and writing their own messages. It is important that children don't waste time on letter games if they already know the letters. Such children are better employed using their knowledge to read and write.

A teacher using *Bumble Bee*[21] for shared reading may focus children's attention on print details in the following way:

- *Point to the title of this book* Bumble Bee *while I read it ...*

- *Listen to the title again. What can you hear that is the same?*

- *Now look at the first letter of each word in the title. What do you notice?*

- *Point to the words on this page (page 2) that begin with the same letter.*

- *Now take out your own alphabet card, the one you use when you're writing.*

- *Which word on your alphabet card begins with the letter b?*

- *When you are writing your own story, this is where you can find the letter b.*

Teachers who are aware of the stages of spelling development (refer to pages 64–9 in *Dancing with the Pen*) can use the student's drafts, and especially the writing approximations, to monitor and develop the student's understanding of:

- the alphabet and letter forms;

- sound-letter relationships;

- principles of direction;

- what a letter is and what a written word is;

- spaces between words;

- letter clusters;

- the order of letters in words;

- the sequence of sounds within words;

- punctuation.

Building a Reading Vocabulary

Skilled readers have learned to recognize many words instantly; they have a large reading vocabulary.

Skilled readers can recognize a large number of words as well as the phrases and patterns in which they occur frequently. As Marie Clay points out, "a child [has] to gradually accumulate a reading vocabulary of known words which [he or she] can recognize rapidly and does not have to work out. Only as this happens is the reader's attention freed to work on new words and solve

---

21 Pat Quinn, *Bumble Bee,* Guided Reading series (Wellington: Learning Media Limited, 1997)

new text problems."[22]   The student gradually acquires reading vocabulary through five main types of activity. These are:

- extensive reading of many kinds of text, using the same reading vocabulary in new and varied settings;

- language experience through shared writing, which makes many spoken words familiar in their written forms, and where new vocabulary is clarified and consolidated;

- the student's own writing, where he or she uses some high-frequency words over and over again, and where experience with these words in their language context is developed as the student rereads what has been written;

- attending to the same words and phrases in many contexts — in notices, on labels and signs, and on television — and noticing environmental print in a variety of situations in the classroom and outside;

- interacting with the teacher, when the teacher selects words from the student's reading and writing to help the student read and write those words fluently.

When students acquire their reading vocabulary through such activities, the printed words and their meanings are learned in natural ways, in the context of reading and writing that has a purpose. Trying to "learn" to read printed words out of context, where their meaning is not clear, can be confusing for students.

During shared or guided reading, students' attention to the reading vocabulary can be developed by focusing on text, using directions and questions such as these.

- *Point to the first word on the page. Look at the first word on the next page.*

- *What can you tell me about those words?*

- *Can you find two words on that page that are the same?*

The teacher then draws students' attention to a recent piece of writing (either a piece from a shared writing session or a piece of work recently

Reading vocabulary is best accumulated through many reading and writing experiences.

I like to ride my bike.

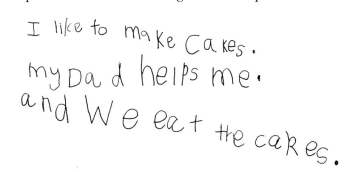

I like to make cakes.
my Dad helps me.
and We eat the cakes.

---

22 *Becoming Literate: The construction of inner control,* p. 183

published by one of the students) and focuses their attention on the same high-frequency words. This helps develop students' understanding of the constancy of print. They realize that the same high-frequency words can be read and written in different contexts.

When the teacher provides modeling and support and uses interesting, high-quality texts, every student discovers enough repetitions of high-frequency words to begin to develop a reading vocabulary. They find many such words as they read and reread their own published writing.

3. *Phonological Patterns*

Students' awareness of the sounds of speech — their phonological awareness — develops naturally within the context of reading, particularly shared reading, where the words are read aloud. Students might talk about similarities between spoken sounds — for example, *house* and *octopus* share the same end sound. At the same time, the students develop their understanding of phonics — knowing how the individual sounds of speech relate to particular symbols in written language.

Activities such as songs, nursery rhymes, and jingles help students develop phonological awareness.

While introducing and discussing texts with individuals or groups, the teacher can focus students' attention on analyzing print. Songs, raps, nursery rhymes, and jingles are very useful for helping students to recognize rhyming words, alliteration, and repetitive structures.

Drawing attention to words and phrases in a story may encourage the students to vary the storyline, incorporating their own ideas and feelings while retaining certain words and phrases. For example, during a second shared reading of the book *Where Are My Socks?*[23] one teacher encouraged the students to discuss the parts of the text that rhymed, such as *cat hat, frog togs,* and *winker blinker.*

Where are my glasses?
Here are my peg legs
But where are my glasses?
Here is my tall ball.
But where are my glasses?
Here is my wink drink.
But where are my glasses?
Here are my glue shoes.
But where are my glasses?
Here is my chicken licken.
But where are my glasses?
And here are my glasses.
But where is my head?

- *Let's say these words together …*

- *Let's look at these words and say them.*

- *Notice how they rhyme.*

Here are my frog togs,   **but where are my socks?**

Following this discussion, the teacher and students together wrote their own version of the text.

---

23 M. Macdonald, *Where Are My Socks?* Guided Reading series (Wellington: Learning Media Limited, 1997)

42

Innovating on text gives students further opportunities to experience the patterns and rhymes of text they have shared. These texts should be accessible to students, either in book form or on the wall at a height where students can easily reread them. Students can use pointers to practice directionality and one-to-one matching.

Linguists use the terms "onset" and "rime" to describe the two parts of single-syllable words that students need to know. The beginning part of the word is called the onset, and the cluster that makes the rhyme in songs, raps, poetry, and jingles is called the rime. For example, in the word "sent," the onset is the consonant "s-," and the rime is the cluster "-ent."

Current research highlights the importance of students having an awareness of the different parts of words.[24] In helping students to refine this awareness, during word analysis work in reading and writing, it is important to remember that children can hear syllables and rimes and that, from rimes, they can discover onsets. Teachers can help them to use this ability in their reading and writing.

Within the context of writing, students can develop their phonological awareness when they are composing their own messages. As students write what they want to say, they can be helped to work out an essential understanding of how what they hear can be recorded using letters. Successful readers focus on the biggest cluster of letters, within a word, that will enable them to read the word.

For the skilled reader, it is the consistencies in spelling patterns or clusters of letters, rather than letter-sound relationships, that assist the reading. Helping beginning readers attend to letter-sound relationships at the start of a word is often an important first step. Drawing attention to orthography or spelling patterns builds students' phonological awareness. Teachers who are aware of the interplay between early reading and writing will help students to discover new ways of exploring language and comparing segments of language, by building on what they can already read and write.

Skilled readers use their knowledge of spelling patterns and letter clusters.

Using Letter Clusters in Reading

Children learning to read need to attend closely to letters or letter clusters[25] to recognize a word, to anticipate, and to confirm their initial response. Skilled readers tend to use clusters of letters, focusing on the largest cluster of letters, within a word, that will enable them to analyze the word most rapidly. The skilled reader recognizes a familiar cluster at once and links it with sounds to produce a response that fits the sense of the passage. As a further check, the reader may ensure that the sounds of the word are represented by letters on the page.

---

24 For example, C. Kirtley, P. Bryant, M. MacLean, and L. Bradley, "Rhythm, Rime, and the Onset of Reading," *Journal of Experimental Child Psychology* 48 (1989): pp. 224–245

25 In this book, "letter cluster" means simply a group of letters that is part of a word.

Using Writing

Children who are writing down what they want to say have to work out how what is heard can be recorded by letters. Writing thus provides opportunities for students to practice hearing sound sequences in words and to associate them with the corresponding letters and letter clusters.

Helping Students Use Letter-sound Relationships — Phonics

Students' knowledge of sound-to-letter correspondences can help them to develop their knowledge of letter-to-sound correspondences.

The strategy of analyzing spoken words into sounds (as when students slowly articulate a word that they are about to write but that they do not know how to spell) and then going from sounds to letters (linking the sounds they can hear to certain letters and writing some of these) may be a precursor to being able to use letter-sound relationships in reading.[26] At the beginning stage of reading, the teacher needs to help the student to make links between sound-to-letter analysis in writing and letter-to-sound analysis in reading. Sound-to-letter analysis skills sometimes precede letter-to-sound analysis, but this situation does not last for very long. Students who have acquired only a small reading and writing vocabulary begin to work out, quite early, that they can apply what they are learning about writing to their reading.

At any stage during shared or guided reading, teachers can isolate a letter (or letter cluster) for special attention. This should be done only when there are opportunities throughout the text to apply and confirm the knowledge of its associated sound. For example, the letter (or cluster) may recur in the same word or in words containing the same letter-sound relationships. Students may be helped to listen and look for initial, medial, or final similarities and differences, in sequences such as these:[27]

<u>tr</u>uck, <u>tr</u>ailer	in *The Biggest Cake in the World*
four <u>b</u>ig <u>b</u>abies	in *Blackbird's Nest*
sch<u>oo</u>l, P<u>oo</u>l	in *Our Teacher, Miss Pool*
b<u>a</u>d, D<u>a</u>d	in *"Smile!" said Dad*
r<u>ea</u>dy, st<u>ea</u>dy	in *Ready, Steady, Jump!*

Teachers can use texts with consonant clusters such as th- and str-, and prefixes and suffixes such as un-, re-, -er, and -ly.

To help students discover letter-sound relationships in selected texts, it is best to work from the known to the unknown by following these steps.

Working from the known to the unknown helps students attend to letter-sound relationships.

1. The student listens to identify the sound.

2. The student looks and listens to identify the written form of the letter and associate it with a sound.

---

26 R. J. Tierney and T. Shanahan, "Research on the Reading-writing Relationship: Interactions, transactions and outcomes," *Handbook of Reading Research 2* (New York: Longman, 1991), pp. 246–280

27 See Guided Reading series (Wellington: Learning Media Limited, 1997)

3. The student attempts to give a similar example from words they already know from reading or everyday speech.

4. The student applies the new knowledge, taking it back into reading the text.

Shared and guided reading provide excellent opportunities for helping students focus on print details and develop their ability to use letter-sound relationships. But in taking such opportunities, teachers should always keep in mind that reading for meaning is paramount in importance. Do not overdo word analysis.

When analyzing and discussing words, use letter names as well as letter sounds. Students can find it very difficult to relate sounds to consonants in isolation, and most vowels represent several sounds. Remember, too, that while letters in the initial position are the most useful for the beginning reader identifying unknown words, students also need to learn to scan words and to attend to letters and groups of letters in other positions.

Working on Chunks or Clusters of Letters

Good readers read in chunks and, where possible, attach sounds to a group of letters rather than to each letter. Students' attention should be directed within words to the largest chunk or cluster of letters that helps them recognize the word. Work on chunks, syllables, compound words, root words, and contractions should take place as examples occur in the context of reading texts and writing messages.

In the following example, a teacher directs a group of students at the early reading stage of a guided reading season. The text is *The Praying Mantis*.[28]

- *Let's look at this word here.* (She writes *munch* on a chart.)

- *What other word on the page looks like "munch"?* (She adds the word *crunch* to the chart.)

- *What is it about these words that is the same?* (During the discussion, the teacher underlines the common chunk.)

- *Do you know of any other words that sound the same? What other word rhymes with "munch" and "crunch"?*

- *Let's write them up here. Can you see the part of these words that is the same? Which part is it?*

Munch, crunch. Munch, crunch.

POW!

---

28 P. Cartwright, *The Praying Mantis,* Guided Reading series (Wellington: Learning Media Limited, 1997)

Integrating the Strategies

Successful readers use and integrate the full repertoire of reading strategies. A student with control over only a few strategies is at a disadvantage and may respond to text in inappropriate ways. Such students may come to rely too much on their memory or on the assistance of others. The teacher needs to identify what students can already do and how they can be helped to take the next step. Students learn to integrate strategies when the teacher:

- provides opportunities for them to work things out for themselves;

- praises them for showing independence;

- focuses on opportunities for them to overcome challenges, asking questions and discussing points in the text with them.

Marie Clay says that teachers aim to produce independent readers, whose reading and writing improve whenever they read and write. When such students are reading:

- early strategies are secure and habituated;

- they monitor their own reading or writing;

- they search for cues in word sequences, in meaning, and in letter sequences;

- they discover new things for themselves;

- they cross-check one source of information with another;

- they repeat, as if to confirm, their reading or writing;

- they self-correct, assuming the initiative for making cues match or getting words right;

- they solve new words by these means.

An Example

In this example, the teacher helps a student who cannot read the word "claws" in the following sentence from *The Hogboggit:* "I see the Hogboggit's claws."[29]

The teacher may refer to the cover and ask an opening question, such as, "What's scary about the Hogboggit here?" The student might anticipate, using the picture and any previous experience. The teacher encourages the student to relate this attempt to the print by saying some of these things:

- *Try reading from the beginning of the sentence again and think what would fit.* (Encourage young children to reread as the first strategy. Rereading helps comprehension.)

- *What does your word begin with? Think of a word that looks right, sounds right, and makes sense.* (Encourage the student to attend to visual information, such as the significant letters of the word, to link this visual information with known items, and to cross-check with meaning.)

---

29 *The Hogboggit,* Guided Reading series (Wellington: Learning Media Limited, 1997)

Teachers need to help students integrate their reading strategies.

Slightly adapted from M. M. Clay, *An Observation Survey of Early Literacy Achievement* (Auckland: Heinemann, 1993), p. 12

Alternatively, the teacher may tell the student the word and, if appropriate, the student can be encouraged to confirm or correct by further questions, such as:

- *Does that make sense?* or *Does that sound right?* (encouraging the student to use meaning and structure to confirm).

- *How can you be sure?* or *How do you know?* (encouraging the student to check and take responsibility for self-correction).

- *Are you happy with that?* (encouraging the student to take responsibility for confirmation).

- *Does that make sense and look right to you?* (encouraging the student to cross-check meaning and visual and phonological information).

- *Would you read that again?* (encouraging the student to check further, put the word back into context, and perhaps self-correct).

- *What's another word that begins with those two letters?* (referring to the familiar letters in another context) — *Let's write some down.*

I see the hogboggit's claws.   It sees *my* claws.

These are the sorts of question that students, in time, will learn to ask and answer for themselves. Such questions are at the heart of a self-extending system in which reading strategies are integrated. The following example shows a student asking and answering a question about the text.

Mum got out
her knitting needles
to knit a woolly jacket.

Child: That should be n-nitting, is it?
Teacher: What do you think?
Child: It is.

At the early stages, a critical role of the teacher is to help students learn to use a network of strategies, attending, anticipating, confirming, and self-correcting where necessary. Teachers do this as they support and guide students through text. Later, the teacher's role changes to one of providing opportunities for the students to expand and extend the range of texts across which their network can operate.

4 Knowing the Learner

What Assessment of Reading Involves

Assessment in reading involves collecting, through a variety of procedures, information about students' skills, understandings, attitudes, interests, and previous learning experiences. Secondly, it involves making informed judgments about students' learning based on this information and then planning accordingly.

> *Assessment of individual students' progress is essentially diagnostic. Such assessment is integral to the teaching and learning program. Its purpose is to improve teaching and learning by diagnosing learning strengths and weaknesses, measuring students' progress against the defined achievement objectives, and reviewing the effectiveness of teaching programs.*[30]

Assessment is integral to the learning and teaching program.

The Purpose of Assessment

The method of assessment and the type of information gathered will depend on the purpose of assessment. Assessment may be done to:

- find out what has already been learned;

- find out how well the student is meeting the reading objectives and what intervention is needed;

- provide constructive feedback to the learner;

- indicate the direction of future teaching and learning;

- select the right materials, approaches, and strategies for the student;

- report to parents;

- enable teachers to match learning experiences to individuals or groups;

- monitor and identify progress over time;

- reflect on teaching practices and organization;

- provide information about class or school achievement.

In a student-centered program, the teacher begins with what a student can already do, sets realistic goals based on individual needs, and then provides learning opportunities to help the student meet these.

Knowing the Student

To assess students' reading progress successfully, teachers need to know the students they teach. "Knowing the student" means more than knowing about the student's reading — it involves knowing the student as an individual. Because reading is a process where information from the text and the student's understanding of the world interact to produce meaning, it is necessary for the teacher of reading to know as much as possible about the student's world.

Information about students' reading development should be collected from a variety of sources.

---

30 *The New Zealand Curriculum Framework*, p. 24

Frank Smith states:

The teacher's role is to motivate, encourage, and help children to read. To do this teachers must make reading meaningful, which means seeing how it looks from the child's point of view. Teachers must understand both children and reading.[31]

One teacher explains how knowing the children is necessary for assessing and supporting reading progress:

Each child brings different experiences and background to their learning. By "knowing" each child and accepting what they bring to their learning, I am able to match material to their needs and support them in their learning. By knowing what they are doing and how they are doing it, and by knowing how children learn, I am able to assist them in moving on in their learning. I can only know my students by observing them individually. I build up a picture of each child that is continually being added to - the information must be up to date. I gather information in many different ways, but the most important factor for me is whether this information and the evaluation of it is going to assist the child with their learning. By knowing my students, I will be aware that some approaches and resources will be more effective than others.

To know the student, the teacher must know the student's culture and background. Students bring a diversity of experiences, cultural values, expectations about print, and personal interests from home, adding richness and vitality to the social climate of the classroom. Teachers need to be sensitive to the diverse cultural and social backgrounds of the children they teach, and to ensure that their own value systems do not influence their expectations of what students can achieve.

> Teachers need to be sensitive to the cultural and social identity of learners.

Attitudes, Understandings, and Behaviors of Developing Readers over Three Broad Overlapping Stages

The lists on the pages that follow are a general guide to the attitudes, understandings, and behaviors of developing readers at the emergent, early, and fluent stages. As readers progress in their reading, they develop and extend the processing strategies, building on what they have learned in previous stages. All stages have common elements, but the emphasis differs.

For easy reference, the understandings and behaviors have been loosely grouped under three headings: Thinking Critically, Exploring Language, and Processing Information.

Thinking Critically requires the reader to interpret, compare, analyze, and evaluate texts, giving their own response to what has been read.

Exploring Language refers to the reader's developing use and understandings of how language works.

Processing Information involves the reader in accessing and using information to confirm meaning, solve problems, and extend experience and knowledge.

---

31   F. Smith, *Reading* (New York: Cambridge University Press, 1978), p. 164

Emergent Readers

Attitudes

The emergent reader:
- enjoys listening to stories;
- wants to participate in reading stories, poems, and rhymes;
- is keen to read and see herself or himself as a reader;
- expects books to be enjoyable, informative, or exciting;
- returns to favorite books;
- expects to understand and respond to texts that are read to or with the group;
- is interested in a range of written texts, both fiction and non-fiction.

Understandings and Behaviors

Thinking Critically

The emergent reader:
- anticipates the storyline;
- uses title and illustrations to anticipate what text might be about;
- is beginning to use sources of information to assist with word recognition;
- attends to meaning, structure, and some print details in texts;
- can understand and discuss the relationship between characters in stories;
- relates own personal experiences to the texts read.

Exploring Language

The emergent reader:
- holds the text, turns pages correctly, and reads from top to bottom;
- knows some print conventions, such as directionality, sentence beginnings and endings, capital letters, rhymes, and word beginnings and endings;
- can distinguish the sound sequence in some words;
- identifies some words;
- recognizes periods, capital letters, and spaces between words;
- recognizes and names some letters of the alphabet, and shows an awareness of letter-sound relationships and rhyme;
- knows that language can be recorded in a variety of forms, including stories, poems, rhymes, letters, labels, instructions, advertisements on television, and so on;
- recognizes and reads familiar signs, labels, and advertising slogans;
- uses terminology like books, print, letters, title, page, cover, illustrations, author, and so on.

Processing Information

The emergent reader:
- expresses personal views about a character's actions and can relate them to their own behavior;
- can retell a story;
- rereads and self-corrects;
- understands that both illustrations and the text carry the message;
- uses pictures as useful clues to meaning;
- can find significant details in the story by using pictures;
- is able to draw pictures describing events in a story or poem;
- uses knowledge of sound-symbol relationships by saying a word aloud while trying to write it;
- responds to a variety of texts such as notices, posters, instructions, and advertising.

Early Readers

Attitudes

The early reader:
- is keen to hear and to read longer books;
- enjoys reading and responding to easy texts;
- is prepared to take risks, and makes approximations;
- likes to visit and use the library;
- expects to construct meaning from an increasing range of texts and illustrations;
- likes to explore new words and language patterns;
- reads for pleasure and information.

Understandings and Behaviors

Thinking Critically

The early reader:
- can comment on aspects of the plot, characters, and sequence of events in a narrative or an account;
- understands that there may be more than one interpretation of a text;
- understands the reader's role in extending context and making inferences;
- likes to discuss favorite books and recommend and share them with others;
- uses illustrations for checking rather than as clues for words;
- relates their own experiences to what is read.

Exploring Language

The early reader:
- has clear concepts about print;
- is developing a considerable reading vocabulary;
- can interpret such markers as question marks, exclamation points, and commas when reading aloud;
- points out organizational features such as paragraphs, headings, diagrams, table of contents, and indexes;
- begins to use punctuation correctly in writing;
- uses sources of information, including phonological awareness, to identify unknown words;
- self-corrects when meaning is lost while reading simple texts;
- knows that texts are written by people and represent real and imaginary experience;
- knows the difference between different types of text, such as diaries, poems, narrative, directions, advertisements, invitations, letters, and notices.

Processing Information

The early reader:
- knows how to find pictures, audiotapes, chapter books, and non-fiction texts in the library and can use the catalog with help;
- can select reading material and gather information on a topic from a variety of sources with help;
- retells a story or ideas from an expository text, providing some detail from the text;
- talks about their own interpretation of information from advertisements;
- is beginning to use a database;
- chooses texts for enjoyment and information on the basis of interest, book cover, illustrations, and recommendation from others;
- responds to an increasing range of texts, such as posters, instructions, articles, plays, descriptions.

Fluent Readers

Attitudes

The fluent reader:
- is keen to select and read independently, and for enjoyment, from a range of contemporary and historical texts;
- pursues reading interests and takes time to read;
- expects to discover new meanings and applications on further reading;
- is critically reflective.

Understandings and Behaviors

Thinking Critically

The fluent reader:
- identifies and discusses the choices authors make;
- can identify and discuss the author's viewpoint;
- recognizes stereotyping, and racist and sexist language;
- discusses topical items on television, in newspapers, and in magazines and relates these critically to their own experience;
- uses evidence from text to support a point of view;
- knows that texts are constructed for different purposes and for different audiences;
- displays confidence in talking about books and authors and can deliver reports, retellings, and summaries confidently;
- can relate the theme of the narrative to their own beliefs and culture.

Exploring Language

The fluent reader:
- uses table of contents, glossary, and index with confidence;
- integrates sources of information efficiently and uses a variety of reading strategies to solve difficulties;
- demonstrates knowledge of the structure of language and of how it works;
- comments intelligently on aspects of fiction, such as plot, characters, and sequences of events, and also on aspects of non-fiction, such as arguments, logical relationships, and viewpoint;
- can discuss the different language features in advertising used to persuade the reader.

Processing Information

The fluent reader:
- uses the library independently and confidently;
- uses databases effectively;
- accesses and uses information from a range of sources;
- can skim read, make notes, and summarize information;
- understands and follows logical sequences in instructions or explanations;
- extracts and uses relevant information for their own purposes as well as for directed tasks;
- reads a wide variety of texts fluently with good comprehension;
- chooses and requests new titles by favorite authors.

Planning for Assessment

Assessing students' needs, and planning programs, are an integral part of teaching and learning in the classroom. The two things go hand in hand — teachers find out about the students and their reading through ongoing assessment, which enables them to plan appropriate programs. The following diagram shows how assessment happens throughout the learning cycle.

The Assessment Learning Cycle

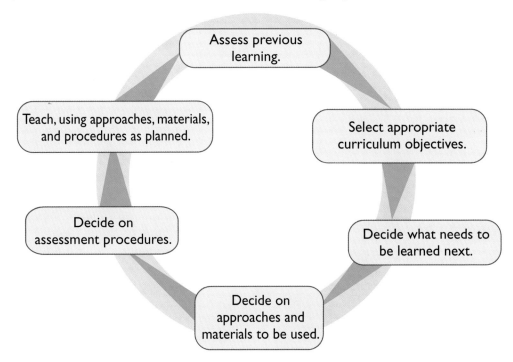

Assessment should be an ongoing and natural part of the reading program.

Assessment should occur naturally and regularly as part of students' learning experiences. Remember that the nature and scope of students' learning varies. Through daily observations of students' reading behavior, the teacher can confirm or modify information gained about them during daily language activities. It is critical that students having difficulties in learning to read are monitored regularly to ensure that they are learning appropriate strategies and behaviors.

Knowing What Procedures to Use

When teachers are choosing which procedures to use, they will consider a range of factors, such as the purpose of the assessment and what is being assessed. The following chart provides some suggestions.

Note: Information about a student can also be gathered from school records, other students, other teachers, and the student's family, as appropriate.

What is Assessed?	Assessment Procedures
attitudes; interests; strategies; knowledge; skills; understandings; range of reading; information processes	*teacher observations; anecdotal records; cumulative files; profiles; standardized tests*
information sources and strategies used; suitability of material to learning needs; understandings; progress over time	*running records; information from student's retellings*
attitudes; interests; knowledge; suitability of texts to interests, needs, and range of reading; ability to articulate understandings; understanding of the language and structure of written texts	*information from conferences with student*
understanding of the process; content knowledge; attitudes; interests; range of reading	*self-assessment, including reading logs or diaries, reading-response journals, personal goals sheets*
summing up individual characteristics and progress	*individual students' portfolios, profiles; progress against curriculum objectives*

Assessment Procedures

Assessment by the Teacher

Because monitoring is such an integral part of the teaching and learning process, it is vital that the person who teaches the student also assesses that student's learning.

The following assessment procedures include a range of approaches that focus on the role of the teacher in the assessment process.

Teacher Observations

Teachers have opportunities to observe students in a variety of reading contexts. Observations range from the informal noting of a new aspect of reading behavior to more systematic and planned observation of the student applying understandings and skills that have been taught.

Although observations can take place at any time, it is important that teachers plan to observe, and have a clear idea of what they are looking for. Often this can be done in group situations, such as guided and shared reading sessions. However, students' reading development need not be observed only in "reading time," since the students will be using their ability to read to meet objectives in other curriculum areas as well. For example, students' ability to gather, select, interpret, and record information from a range of resources may be observed in science.

Records of teacher observations form a valuable source of information about students' reading. Planning and managing observation effectively is a challenge for the teacher in a dynamic classroom. Teachers need to plan to focus on particular students within a particular time frame. Where significant behaviors

3.10 Independent reading: enthusiastic brings books from home. Often helps in the library at lunchtime.

4.5 Guided Reading: used title and illustrations to make predictions. She offers a range of opinions, supported these with extracts from the text.

is comfortable with different interpretations

4.20 Shared 'Grandpa's Cardigan' with the class. — enjoyed the humor in the text.

4.26 Used card index in library to find book: needed help.

Teacher observations of eight-year-old Emma's reading show she chooses to read whenever possible, selects her own reading material, and often brings books from home. Most of the books she chooses are fiction in the form of picture books, although she is currently reading her first novel. In guided and shared reading, she demonstrates she can: make predictions about the texts; bring her background experiences to the text; offer points of view in discussion; and re-evaluate her point of view in light of what others say. She is beginning to notice, and make comments about, the structure of texts.

are observed (for example, those that indicate change), they should be recorded anecdotally, to guide further teaching and add to the student's ongoing record. One way of doing this is to record comments in a small notebook. Another way is to use a sheet of paper ruled into squares, one for each student. Comments need to be updated regularly.

Running Records

Running records provide an accurate and objective description of oral reading behavior.

Running records are a way of observing, scoring, and analyzing students' reading behavior.[32] They provide information on:

- strategies students use to build meaning;
- how readers process information;
- how readers use different sources of information to solve unfamiliar words;
- whether the difficulty level of the text is appropriate;
- the student's willingness to take risks;
- how students integrate the strategies during independent reading;
- whether students are choosing appropriate text levels for independent reading.

The text chosen for a running record should be one that the student has read before in guided reading. Occasionally a teacher will choose a text the student has not seen.

32 For a detailed description of taking, scoring, and analyzing running records, see Marie Clay's book *An Observation Survey of Literacy Achievement*, cited previously.

Learning to take running records requires some practice, but the quality of information provided about a student's reading behavior makes it worthwhile.

A teacher takes a running record by sitting alongside a student so that the text the student is reading can be easily seen. The teacher records everything the student says and does while the student reads the text aloud. Recording can be done on a pro forma record sheet like the one shown on page 58, or on a blank piece of paper — "even the back of a bus ticket," Marie Clay once declared.

Ways of recording students' reading behavior are as follows:

1. Accurate reading
Every word read correctly is marked with a check. ✓ ✓ ✓ ✓

2. Substitution
All attempts and errors are shown by recording them with text underneath.

✓ ✓ ✓ ✓ g / r / games   *(one error)*
             cards

If a student tries several times to read a word, record all trials. If the trial results in a correct word, it is not an error.

3. Omission
If a word is left out, or there is no response to it, record it with a dash.

—
cards   *(one error)*

4. Insertion
If a word is inserted, it is recorded over a dash.

large   *(one error)*
—

5. Told
When the reader makes no attempt at the word or cannot continue, ask the reader to try, but if the student is still stuck, tell the student the word.

—
garbage | T   *(one error)*

6. Appeal or Told
If the student appeals for help, turn the problem back to the student by saying, "You try it." If the student cannot continue, tell the student the word.

— | A |
garbage | T   *(one error)*

7. Self-correction
The symbol "sc" is used to record a self-correction immediately after the error. Note: If a substitution is self-corrected, no error is scored.

✓✓ the | sc
     and | *(one self-correction)*

8. Repetition
Repetition is not counted as an error, but it should be shown because it often results in a self-correction.

✓ ✓ ga gar | R₂ | Sc
     garden | *(one self-correction)*

RUNNING RECORD SHEET

Name: _____ Date: _____ D. of B.: _____ Age: ____ yrs ____ mths

School: _____ Recorder: _____

Text Titles	Running words Error	Error rate	Accuracy	Self-correction rate
1. Easy _____ _____		1: _____	____ %	1: _____
2. Instructional HURRY, HURRY, HURRY (S) $\frac{16\cancel{4}}{11}$		1: 15	93 %	1: 2
3. Hard _____ _____		1: _____	____ %	1: _____

Directional movement ✓ _____

Analysis of Errors and Self-corrections
Information used or neglected [Meaning (M) Structure or Syntax (S) Visual (V)]

Easy _____

Instructional Meaning and structure cues are used predominantly for substitutions with limited attention to visual cues. Does not attempt some words. Self corrects using visual cues

Hard _____

Cross-checking on information (Note that this behavior changes over time)

Meaning and structure cues appear to be cross-checked with visual information on some occasions.   Analysis of Errors and Self-corrections

Page	HURRY HURRY HURRY (CRINKUM CRANKUM)	E	SC	Information used E MSV	SC MSV
8	✓ ✓ ✓ ✓ almost ✓ ✓ hearly	I		(M)(S)v	
9	✓ ✓ ✓ ✓ ✓ ✓ ✓ ✓ ✓ f ✓ ✓ ✓ ✓ final				

10	✓ ✓ ✓ ✓ ✓ ✓
	n ✓ ✓ ✓ y SC ✓
	now that
	↓ ✓ ✓ R — R ✓ ✓ ✓ ✓
	        drink T
	✓ ✓ ✓ R — R ✓ ✓
	        shake T
		I
		I
		I
			I	(M)(S)V
				MSV
				MSV
					M S(V)

Sometimes a student gets into a muddle. The best way to extricate the student is to say, "Try that again," showing the student where to begin. This is counted as one error only, and then a normal record is made of the fresh beginning.

Scoring Running Records

The accuracy rate can be calculated by dividing the number of words read by the number of errors, which gives a ratio of errors to correct words read. A table is used to convert this ratio to a percentage of accuracy. For example, one error in ten running words means that the reader is reading at a 90% accuracy rate, the minimum for successful guided reading.

The self-correction rate is calculated by adding both errors and self-corrections, and dividing by the number of self-corrections.

If the text is too difficult, the reader's accuracy rate and the self-correction rate will be low. The accuracy and self-correction rates provide an indication of how challenging or easy the text was and of whether the teacher's introduction to the text provided sufficient support for successful reading. When the challenges in the text become too great for the reader, the reading process breaks down, with the result that only one or two sources of information are used.

Analyzing Running Records

Taking a running record is the first step. Analyzing the running record is the second. Only when a careful analysis has been carried out can the teacher plan effectively for the student's next learning step. Analysis of running records involves examining each attempt and self-correction and deciding which sources of information the reader was using at the point of error or self-correction. This is done by circling the initial letter of the cues used (meaning, structural, and visual) for both errors and self-corrections. See the examples provided.

When analyzing their records of a student's reading, teachers should ask themselves these questions:

- Is the student trying to make sense of what is being read? (meaning information)

- Is knowledge of language patterns being used? (structural information)

- Is knowledge of the letter-sound relationships being used? (phonic information)

- Is knowledge of letters, words, and print conventions being used? (visual information)

- Are confirmation and self-correcting strategies being used?

Note: To make running records easier to follow, in this book the reader's responses have been transcribed above the text.

Fun With Mo and Toots

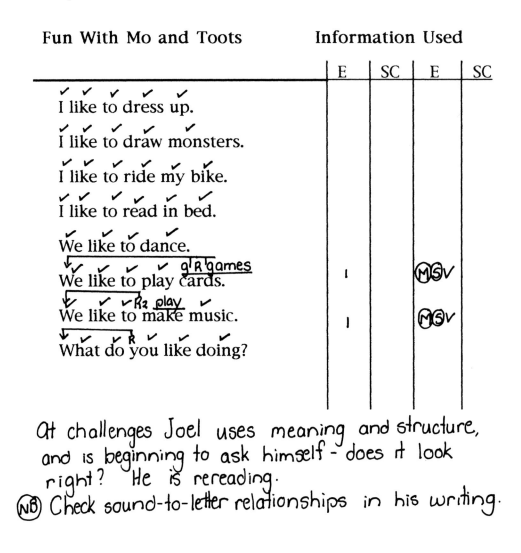

At challenges Joel uses meaning and structure, and is beginning to ask himself - does it look right? He is rereading.

(NB) Check sound-to-letter relationships in his writing.

When making decisions about Joel's next learning step, his teacher also used information from his latest writing sample.

(I have got six kittens.)

Joel's understanding of the relationship between sounds and letters was evident in this piece of writing. The partial phonetic representation of each spelling approximation shows his growing control of alphabet knowledge and the degree to which he understands that sounds in words can be represented by letters. While Joel's understanding of sound-to-letter relationships was developing, his teacher decided that his next step would be learning to make letter-to-sound associations when he met unfamiliar words in reading. She planned to achieve this by helping Joel attend to visual and phonological information — beginning with the first letter of the word.

If the analysis of the running record shows that the student is not consistently using the sources of information and strategies in an integrated way, the teacher can then provide guidance. The chapters on Developing the Strategies and Knowing the Approaches give suggestions for teachers about this.

This further example shows how a running record accurately identifies strategies being used in reading and also serves as a check on writing skills .

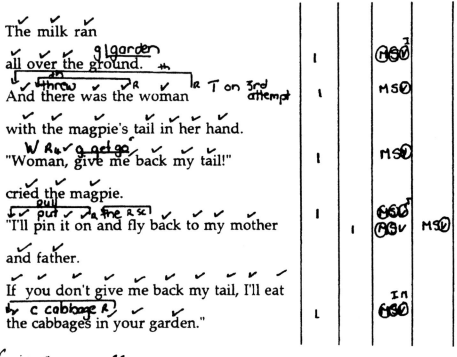

Sori:
- generally used meaning at challenging words and often used structure;
- when approximating she usually checked further, often by rereading, and this led to a number of self-corrections;
- her approximations show she is mainly using initial letters and she needs to search further;
- she reads with phrasing and retold the story confidently.

N.B. Check out spelling approximations in writing!

Running records can be an excellent method of monitoring reading development with older students who are still learning to use strategies independently. This running record of ten-year-old Claire reading "The Burglar" (*School Journal*, Part 4 Number 3, 1989) indicates what should be her next learning step.

"Because I'm years older," Hannah smirked.

He gave up arguing and stomped off towards his bedroom. She room. "See you in the morning," he said to his mother to emphasize that he was ignoring Hannah.

He posed in front of his bedroom mirror. If Hannah was a damsel in distress, she couldn't expect him to come galloping to her rescue. She could stay tied to the stake. He would charge in, cutting this way and that with his fearsome sword. All would fall before him and he would fight his way to where she was tied. He danced across his room, swinging his arm from side to side.

Claire • uses meaning, structure, and visual sources
  • rereads occasionally
  • self-corrects most of her errors, usually by using visual information
  • attempts all words

Claire needs to take responsibility for making all the sources of information match.
She needs to be encouraged to recognize when meaning is lost and self-correct.

When used with fluent readers, running records like Emma's (shown on the next page) may confirm that students are using a range of strategies and integrating the sources of information independently. However, running records like this are unlikely to provide useful information for deciding on the students' next learning steps. This information will need to be collected using other assessment strategies.

resting their elbows on it, and talking over its head. "Very uncomfortable for the Dormouse," thought Alice; "only ~~as~~ it's asleep, I suppose it doesn't mind."

I		Ⓜ Ⓢ V

The table was a large one, but the three were all crowded together at one corner of it. "No room! No room!" they cried out when they saw Alice coming. "There's plenty of room!" said Alice indignantly, and she sat down in a large arm-chair at one end of the table.

indently

I		M S Ⓥ

"Have some wine," the March Hare said in an encouraging tone.

Alice looked around the table but there was nothing but tea. "I don't see any wine," she remarked.

"There isn't any," said the March Hare.
"Then it wasn't very civil of you to offer it," said Alice angrily.

I		M S Ⓥ

Emma read fluently with phrasing.
She was able to retell the passage but said she found it difficult because it was too near the beginning of a chapter to know what was going to happen.
Civil & indignantly are not words Emma uses in her spoken language.

Emma's running records show that on easy texts she uses sources of information from meaning and structure to anticipate words. She is monitoring her reading, and she self-corrects all errors that affect meaning. Even texts that Emma found challenging provide little or no information on her next area of need. Neither of the two errors Emma made on the second running record were words that she uses in her oral language. She was, however, able to explain that she found the text difficult because it was near the beginning of a chapter and she had not yet read enough to know what was going to happen.

Assessment through Informal Retellings

Retelling can provide a quick check on comprehension.

Analysis of running records does not always give a clear picture of whether the student gathers meaning from the text as a whole. The best way of finding out about a student's comprehension is to ask the student. Having students retell what they have just read gives a quick guide as to how well they understood the text.

Teachers may need to prompt or ask questions to focus the student's attention on certain points or ideas in the text. Where the student has misunderstood the text, the teacher can provide help and clarify a particular meaning. Retelling as a check on comprehension is an informal procedure that often follows the taking of a running record.

Assessment through Conferences

Students should expect to discuss their reading with their teacher.

Conferences are discussions between student and teacher. They are particularly useful for gathering information on the student's successes and for diagnosing any difficulties the student may be having. They can take place at any time and are particulary valuable for monitoring independent reading. Conferences may involve discussing the plot of a book, books that are similar, or the style of writing in an article. Such discussions can provide a valuable picture of the skills and reading interests of a particular student.

Conferences may be with individual students or with a group. Either way, it is important to focus on what students have achieved and are learning to do, rather than on what they have not yet achieved. Teachers can use reading conferences for a range of purposes, for example, to help students:

- select material to read;

- focus on gathering meaning;

- focus on what they are trying to learn;

- focus on the language features of texts;

- locate and use information from texts;

- learn to set goals for themselves.

The questions teachers ask should provide good models for the questions students should be beginning to ask themselves (like those on page 65).

Written records, and other information from conferences, can be put into the student's cumulative file (refer to page 66).

Information collected from a number of conferences with Emma reveals that she is confident about her reading, and she describes herself as a very good reader. She knows there are texts that she would find difficult to read, but she sees the difficulty as lying within the text. Difficult texts have "small print," "long sentences," or "words I don't know the meaning of."

Emma can identify patterns in her writing that come from her reading, for example, "Once upon a time." Emma describes the process she uses to read as "when I come to a word I don't know, I write it down and then ask somebody." However, her running records show she uses sources of information well. Emma chooses her own books and can describe the types of books she likes. She does not choose to read expository texts but can identify and describe the text features of some genres (instructions, narratives). This is reflected in her own writing.

Self-assessment

When students assess themselves, they are showing their independence. Self-assessment is also a powerful way of motivating students to learn more. Students who are involved in setting their own objectives and monitoring and evaluating their own progress develop insights into their own learning.

Often, self-assessment in reading begins when a student is encouraged to ask *Does it make sense? Can I say it that way? Does it look right?* as they attempt to read an unknown word. Students can be encouraged to reflect upon their progress and ask themselves questions such as:

Self-assessment often begins when students begin to self-correct their attempts.

- *What am I learning to do?*

- *What is the purpose for the reading?*

- *What do I do if the text is too difficult?*

- *How do I go about finding information in printed texts?*

- *What did I learn from what I read?*

- *What do I need help with?*

- *What do I do when I need help?*

- *Can I set my own goals?*

- *What can I do now that I couldn't do before?*

Sometimes students' concepts about what makes a good reader are different from the teacher's, and it is important that teachers are aware of these differences. A student who believes that fluent reading means reading aloud with expression is unlikely to see rereading and self-correcting behaviors as positive signs of growth.

READING CONFERENCE CARD

Maria

I AM LEARNING TO:		I CAN:	
2/14	Discuss an author's writing style (Gary Poulson)	2/17	Read instructions and say whether they are clear or not
3/2	Compare books by two authors (Gary Poulson and Cynthia Voight)	3/5	Find the main idea in a paragraph
3/10	Read and compare different diaries	3/16	Compare books by 2 authors (book review)
3/30	Find all kinds of information about one topic, in the school library		

Self-evaluations can be recorded by the teacher as anecdotal notes or by the student in the form of a reading log, written evaluation, or personal goals sheet.

Reading-response journals or logs can be used by students at all levels of the school to record details of the books they read and to make comments about them. They provide a useful resource for teachers who want to ascertain students' reading interests and find out how many books they are reading.

Emma's own assessment of her reading is that she is a good oral reader because "I try hard to make it interesting for other people." She believes she is a good reader of, and listener to, stories because she finds it "easy" to understand what they are about. Emma's recent goal for herself in reading was to read a chapter book, and she has done this.

School Entry Checks

Teachers begin collecting and recording information about students and their development in reading from the time they enter school. By the time a student has been at school for a month, the teacher should have gathered sufficient information about the student's abilities and interests to lay a foundation for further action.

The Observation Survey

The Observation Survey of Early Literacy Achievement[33] describes six measures for observing students who have been at school for a year. It is completed in association with observations teachers make in the course of their teaching. The observation tasks include: taking running records, checking on students' letter identification and concepts about print, giving word tests, and giving dictation to check how students are writing and hearing sounds in words. These observation tasks provide diagnostic information about a student's strengths and what needs to be learned next.

What to Do with Assessment Information

The information collected through ongoing assessment is of little value unless it is used to assist students' learning.

The information should be kept in a cumulative file and reviewed regularly to check students' progress. Only relevant information should be filed.

The Cumulative File or Portfolio

By keeping cumulative files or portfolios, a teacher can document students' reading development over time. The portfolio should include both qualitative (descriptive) information and quantitative information, such as test results.

---

33 For further information, refer to Marie Clay's book, *An Observation Survey of Early Literacy Achievement* (Auckland: Heinemann, 1993)

Both the student and the teacher should be responsible for deciding what should go in the file. Running records, records of books read, results of tests, and teacher's notes could be included. When deciding what to keep, consider the usefulness of the information in showing development. Folios of work need to be well organized and regularly updated.

Dated and annotated samples of the student's draft writing as well as selected published writing should be included. These provide valuable insights into the student's understandings of the conventions of print and the structure of texts. The reading conference card (see page 65) can be used for both reading and writing; it can be kept in the student's draft writing book or language portfolio. The student can bring the card to any reading situation with the teacher. After a teaching session, the student or the teacher can record the objective explored on the card for future reference. This gives the student a clear focus for learning.

Portfolios provide clear evidence for the teacher's evaluation of students' learning, which enables teachers to be accountable. In fact, the contents of the portfolio will demonstrate the effectiveness of the teacher's teaching as well as the student's learning. Looking through the file together can provide a very useful starting point for discussions with students (and their parents) about their strengths and next learning steps.

Students and teachers should share the responsibility for deciding what should be included in the cumulative file.

Individual Profiles

The information that each teacher gathers about the student can be summed up in a form that provides a clear profile of the student's overall achievement level in reading.

An example for Emma follows:

In summing up Emma's reading development:

Emma enjoys reading and sees herself as a successful reader. She lists reading as one of her hobbies. She reads fluently and has a range of strategies she uses successfully when faced with challenges. Because Emma monitors her own reading effectively, she is readily able to reread and self-correct when meaning is lost.

Emma reads a range of material, chooses her own books, and actively selects books that interest her. She has two authors she particularly enjoys. She uses the card index in the school library and is able to use the CD-ROM catalog in the public library, with help.

Emma enjoys talking about what she reads. Her comments indicate that she understands the author's message, and she is beginning to make comparisons between texts.

Emma is beginning to gather information from expository texts and use this information. She can use indexes and tables of contents to locate information in texts.

Emma is a fluent reader. She is still showing some characteristics of an early reader on some expository texts.

5 Knowing the Approaches

A Variety of Approaches

To meet the diverse needs of students in any class, teachers need to use a variety of approaches in their teaching of reading. Teachers should plan for:

- reading aloud;

- shared reading and writing;

- guided reading;

- independent reading.

A reading program should provide a range of experiences and approaches.

Each of these approaches offers unique opportunities for the teacher to increase students' skill as confident, competent readers and encourage greater responsibility for independent learning. These approaches can be used at any level in the school.

In most classrooms, teachers will use all or a number of these approaches every day. Each of these approaches offers a different level of support to the student. For example, shared reading provides a great deal of teacher support for the students, whereas in independent reading, students read without any support.

The degree of teacher support will vary depending on the challenges provided by the text.

The following diagram shows how teacher support and student input vary according to the approach and stage of the student's reading development. As readers progress, they become increasingly independent and are able to meet increasing challenges in text.

Teaching Approaches

Challenges for Fluent Readers

As students develop into fluent readers, important changes occur in their reading patterns. Their reading vocabulary increases in parallel with their growing experience and knowledge of the world. They read more kinds of text. Expository texts become more significant to them, both at school and in their lives outside school, as they pursue hobbies and interests. They become more confident about linking ideas together in complex ways and about using specialized vocabulary when it is required. Fluent readers can handle the jargon of familiar interests with ease. (Talking to a young enthusiast about computers, skateboarding, or music will quickly confirm this.) Teachers can tap into this burgeoning expertise and extend the students' reading experience by encouraging them to read texts related to these special interests.

Fluent readers will still need guidance through more challenging texts.

Fluent readers still need support, especially when they are faced with texts that introduce new concepts, specialized vocabulary, or complex language structures. For example, an eleven-year-old fluent reader reading the leading article of a newspaper may need the same degree of guidance as a six-year-old early reader reading a simple text like *Rosa at the Zoo*.[34] In general, however, emergent readers need more teacher support.

Deciding on the Approach

A teacher planning a reading session should give careful consideration to the students' experiences and understandings, the features of the text chosen, and the purpose for the reading.

A text may be used flexibly, for shared reading with one group, guided reading with another, and independent reading by some students.

Teachers who are closely in touch with the students' reading development can make use of the approaches in flexible and effective ways. When deciding which approach to take, teachers need to consider the ratio of supports to challenges in relation to the learner and text.

- If the challenges considerably outweigh the supports, the text is best READ ALOUD or SHARED WITH students, or left until later.

- If there is a manageable degree of challenge, with supports for the readers to facilitate new learning, then GUIDED READING can be used.

- If there are many more supports than challenges in the text, it should be suitable for INDEPENDENT READING.

Reading Aloud

Reading aloud to students is important at all levels. It provides enjoyable experiences of written language, which can be used as a basis for further development. When students have opportunities to listen to a wide range of texts and to see others enjoying reading, it helps them to:

Reading aloud to students enables them to experience texts that they are not yet able to read for themselves.

- become aware of the enjoyment of reading;

- extend their understanding and experience of their world;

- understand that the language of books is different from spoken language;

- develop understanding of the patterns and structures of written language;

- learn new words and ideas;

---

34 J. Cowley, *Rosa at the Zoo*, Guided Reading series (Wellington: Learning Media Limited, 1997)

- give a critical response to a variety of texts;

- develop listening comprehension;

- find out about new writers;

- learn about, and locate models of, particular genres or forms of writing;

- be aware of written texts as sources of information for other curriculum areas;

- see the importance of fluent, well-paced, oral reading.

Reading aloud to students should be a regular feature in all classrooms.

The purpose of reading aloud is to involve students in "a good read," rather than doing any direct teaching. Listening to texts read aloud should be a stimulating and interesting learning experience. Occasionally, the teacher may interrupt the flow of the reading to invite a response to a particular aspect of the story. However, interruptions should be kept to a minimum so that the flow is unhindered and meaning is not lost.

When teachers read non-fiction texts to students, a different kind of interaction may be required. The teacher can draw students' attention to particular features, such as a point of view, the logic of an argument, or the kinds of words being used.

Texts for reading to students should be selected carefully. Teachers may need to practice reading aloud so that they read expressively and interestingly.

Shared Reading

Developed by Holdaway[35], shared reading is an approach where the teacher and a group or class read a text together. It is an essential and joyful component of the daily literacy program, especially in the early grades. The teacher reads the text aloud so that each student, regardless of their ability, is engaged in the reading process and enjoys the text. All students should be able to see the text clearly. A text may be reread by the teacher and children many times over several weeks or during the year. During each rereading of the text, children take more responsibility for reading the text themselves.

Shared reading builds on children's early experience of written texts in the home and community.

A shared-reading session can last for up to thirty minutes each day. It usually involves rereading several familiar texts for enjoyment, modeling reading strategies, and introducing and reading a new text. Shared reading involves

---

35   D. Holdaway, *The Foundations of Literacy* (Sydney: Ashton Scholastic, 1979)

discussion before, during, and after the reading. It allows for a high degree of interaction where opinions, ideas, and interpretations are shared and exchanged. All shared reading texts should be available for students to reread independently.

For older students, shared reading provides support to make difficult texts accessible to all students in a group or class. The emphasis will not be on making anticipations at the word level but rather on supporting students as they interpret and analyze more challenging texts. Shared reading can be used for reading in other curriculum areas, particularly expository texts. In shared reading, all students — including those for whom English is another language — can participate confidently because they are able to construct their own meaning through the illustrations and the shared reading of the text, with the support of the teacher and other readers.

Shared reading provides opportunities for teachers to model fluent reading. It also provides opportunities to show students how to use strategies to integrate meaning and how to use structural and visual cues to solve unknown words. These ideas can be talked about easily and naturally during the reading.

Shared reading:

- introduces young children to the language used in books;

- extends students' knowledge and experience about the world;

- enables all students to join in and share an enjoyable reading experience;

- demonstrates to students what fluent reading sounds like;

- develops a sense of community in the classroom;

- helps students become familiar with texts so they can read independently;

- helps students use and learn to interpret illustrations, diagrams, and charts;

- provides a context for discussing meanings in written texts by using students' background knowledge and experiences;

- increases vocabulary knowledge;

- provides opportunities for teachers to model appropriate reading strategies and how to use meaning, structural, and visual cues, including letter-sound relationships;

- enables teachers to identify and discuss with students the conventions, structures, and language features of written texts;

- gives teachers opportunities to model and practice information skills;

- enables students to learn to distinguish between fiction and non-fiction texts;

- helps students anticipate happenings in the story or development in the topic.

Texts chosen for shared reading should include both fiction and non-fiction. Enlarged texts (big books) have made it possible to use this approach in most schools. Other texts, such as poems and rhymes, can be enlarged by hand on large sheets or on overhead projector transparencies. Large-print class stories, made by the children, provide a valuable source of reading material for shared reading. It is also possible to use individual copies of small books, with the students reading along with the teacher. However, this method lacks a strong central focus.

The key elements of a shared reading session are:

- **choosing** an appropriate text;

- **introducing** the text;

- **reading** the text;

- **discussing** the reading;

- **evaluating** the session and deciding on the need to revisit the text.

Choosing an Appropriate Text

Texts chosen for shared reading should always be worth reading and rereading. Consideration is given to the students' stage of development and the purpose for reading. For example, emergent readers need stories with strong story lines, rich language, and bright, energetic pictures. They need rhymes, stories with a pattern, or poems with humor and warmth. These texts can also be used to teach and model reading strategies, such as directionality and one-to-one word matching.

An emerging reader "needs a battery of books that he or she can zoom through with joyous familiarity."[36] By sharing texts with students in many ways, teachers can tease out understandings and make the books so familiar that most of the students will be able to read them for themselves.

For older fluent readers, a poem or a persuasive piece of writing can be chosen and copied on to a transparency for study and analysis by a group or class. A science text can be chosen for shared reading with a mixed group of sixth grade students so that all students can take part in an experiment.

The goal of shared reading is to help children understand the text so that they can enjoy and learn from it.

---

36 Bill Martin Jr. and Peggy Brogan, *Teacher's Guide to the Instant Readers* (New York: Holt Rinehart and Winston, Inc., 1972), p. 4

The teacher chooses texts that:

- have print large enough to be seen easily by all the children in the group;

- represent a range of genres;

- are enjoyable and informative, and worthwhile to read;

- are new and/or familiar to students;

- can be read right through in about ten minutes or less;

- require using particular reading strategies that lead to problem solving and to fluent reading.

The ultimate goal is always to help students understand the text so that they can enjoy and learn from it.

Introducing the Text

When a new text is chosen, the teacher introduces the text by helping students "tune in" to the story or topic. This introduction should be brief, should involve discussion of the title, pictures, and author, and should relate the ideas in the text to the students' own experiences.

If the text to be shared was *Snap! Splash!*[37] the teacher might say:

- *Does anyone know what sort of bird is in the photograph on the cover?*

- *Do you think the story is likely to be true?*

- *Have a close look at the photographs of the heron. What kind of place do you think it lives in?*

- *What do you think the book is going to tell us about the heron? Let's read and find out.*

Before reading, it is useful for teachers to share with the students the particular strategy being modeled or focused on during the reading so that the students can concentrate on it during the reading — for example, learning to check a word by using visual information.

Reading the Text

The teacher leads the reading of the text. With emergent readers, the teacher uses a pointer to point to each word as it is read. This both helps children attend to the print and models directionality and one-to-one matching. With older students, it is not necessary to point to every word. However, the pointer is used to draw attention to words, information, and various text features.

---

37 J. Buxton, *Snap! Splash!* Guided Reading series (Wellington: Learning Media Limited, 1997)

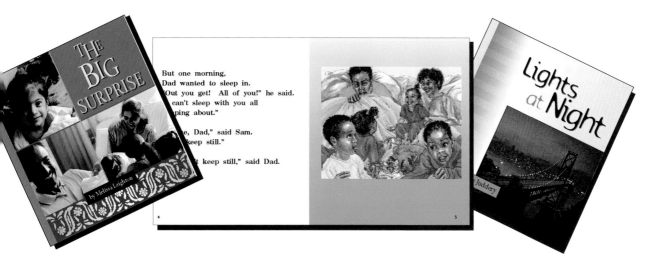

With some texts, children can be invited to join in the first reading, particularly on texts with a catchy refrain or repetitive pattern. Young children will delight in rereading familiar texts with the teacher.

It is during the rereadings that the teacher can model many of the strategies, especially when working with a small group. Strategies, such as using letter-sound relationships, using pictures to predict words and meanings, and checking one source of information against another to make sure the word looks right and sounds right, can be effectively taught during shared reading (see pages 36–45). Removable stickers can be used to cover up words or letters to help students use sources of information other than just the visual information to solve words.

Discussing the Reading

During and after the reading of the text, there will be opportunities for discussing the text and for questions from both the teacher and the children. This interaction should not detract from the fluent reading of the text but rather should complement and enrich the reading. The aim is always to help the children make sense of the text.

Having an easel and chart paper near is essential when discussing and trying to solve new or unfamiliar words or when looking at spelling patterns and other features of text. For older fluent readers, easels are valuable for charting and recording of plot, theme, character development, main ideas or point of view in an article, or information from non-fiction texts.

Evaluating the Session

Shared reading provides a valuable opportunity to observe and listen to students interacting with the text. At the emergent stage, teachers can note children's growing understanding of how print works, observing who is focusing on the text, who is quick to join in with the reading, and who asks questions about the text. This information can be used when deciding on the text and focus for the next shared reading session.

Shared reading with older fluent readers can provide useful information about students' reading development, including, for example: comprehension, vocabulary development, knowledge about structure and features of texts, familiarity with different genres, and the ability to read discerningly and analytically.

Shared Reading with Younger Fluent Readers — an Example

Many stories that are suitable for sharing at the fluency stage encourage readers to consider style, relationships, stories from other places and other times, and different perspectives of literature. In this example, shared reading of *Maui and the Sun*[38] is used to help the students become aware of some features of myths and legends. During discussion before and after the reading, the teacher emphasizes that such stories come from an oral tradition and are sometimes used to explain natural phenomena and highlight human relationships.

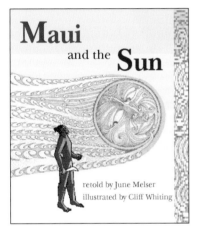

Maui
and the Sun

retold by June Melser
illustrated by Cliff Whiting

Introducing the Text

The teacher encourages students to discuss the cover and explains that the story is a retelling. The concept of retelling can introduce the students to the word "legend." Discussion about the illustration can lead the students to anticipate what the story is about.

Reading the Text

The reading should reflect the pace of the story — it should not be interrupted by too much discussion. The students should be given time to consider the images of action and strength shown in the pictures, as well as the rich book language.

Discussing the Reading

The students could also consider the style of the illustrations and their significance in relation to this story. Other forms and styles of indigenous art could be viewed and discussed. The students could visit the library to find legends from their own and other cultures. Note that the structure of legends varies from culture to culture — European tradition, for instance, favors groups of three, happy endings, and the resolution of problems. Other cultures see the world differently.

The students should be given opportunities to express their reactions to the story through a variety of creative activities. They could try:

• dramatizing the story;

• identifying with one of the characters through creative drama;

---

38 J. Melser, *Maui and the Sun*, Guided Reading series (Wellington: Learning Media Limited, 1997)

- creating music to portray the action of the brothers pulling the sun or of Maui beating the sun;

- exploring patterns through various art media;

- retelling the story in another form, for example, a play or a poem;

- retelling the story from the point of view of one of the characters.

Shared Reading with Older Fluent Readers — an Example

Let the Celebrations Begin! by Margaret Wild and Julie Vivas[39] has a simple text and is a story about the women and children in Belsen. For fluent readers, the challenge is to bring sufficient background knowledge to the reading to take in, and make explicit, certain understandings that are only implied in the text.

The illustrations are hauntingly beautiful and give power to the text, but students may need help in making these links. Teachers sharing this book with students would need to begin by discussing the setting of the story and talking about who the characters are likely to be.

Let the Celebrations Begin! provides an excellent opportunity to explore some of the choices writers make. The text includes examples of three kinds of text on the same topic, written for different purposes and using different genres:

- a very brief explanation in the introduction, using a passive verb;

- the main body of the text, written in narrative in the present tense;

- a personal recount by an eyewitness, at the end of the book and written in the past tense.

Some questions to consider could be the following:

- *The story is told in the present tense. Who is the writer telling the story to?*

- *Why does the writer use dashes and short repetitive phrases?*

- *Why does Miriam sometimes use "we" and at other times "the women and I"?*

The readers could explore these differences and relate them to why and how the different texts were written.

With shared reading, difficult texts become accessible to all children in the class.

Shared Reading across the Curriculum

Shared reading as a means to learning has been field-tested and researched in New Zealand classrooms. The research shows that regular use of shared reading across the curriculum can increase students' motivation to learn, as well as improving their reading in other areas of the curriculum.[40] Because it provides a setting for co-operative learning experiences and pools the expertise of several minds, shared reading can enhance students' appreciation of text as a source of information as well as deepening their knowledge.

Shared reading allows for a high degree of interaction.

39 M. Wild and J. Vivas, *Let the Celebrations Begin!* (Norwood, South Australia: Omnibus Books, 1991)
40 W. B. Elley, *Lessons Learned from LARIC* (Christchurch: University of Canterbury, 1988)

Students will often need support when reading expository texts. These texts often present some unique reading difficulties. Shared reading is an ideal way of providing support for readers to help overcome the challenges in these texts. Teachers will need to model the kinds of questions a good reader asks about particular kinds of expository writing, so that students learn how to cope. Students also need to learn about the linguistic markers that are important in many expository texts — words and phrases such as "moreover," "therefore," or "one reason is."

The article "How to play Ô làng"[41] is an example of a text that may need to be shared first to help students follow the instructions. The use of the conditional ("if ..., then ...") and anaphoric references ("**that** player," "**that** side of the board") mean that keeping track of the sequences described in the text can be quite a challenge for the reader.

The teacher's introductory questions should focus on helping students to anticipate the language structures they are likely to meet, rather than on what the text may be about. The teacher could say, "This text tells us how to play a game" and could then ask:

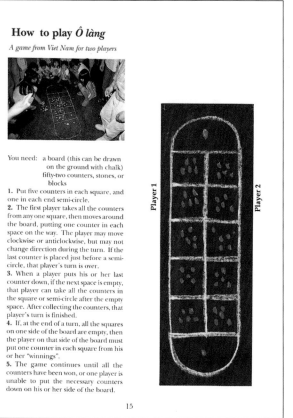

How to play Ô làng

A game from Viet Nam for two players

You need: a board (this can be drawn on the ground with chalk) fifty-two counters, stones, or blocks

1. Put five counters in each square, and one in each end semi-circle.
2. The first player takes all the counters from any one square, then moves around the board, putting one counter in each space on the way. The player may move clockwise or anticlockwise, but may not change direction during the turn. If the last counter is placed just before a semi-circle, that player's turn is over.
3. When a player puts his or her last counter down, if the next space is empty, that player can take all the counters in the square or semi-circle after the empty space. After collecting the counters, that player's turn is finished.
4. If, at the end of a turn, all the squares on one side of the board are empty, then the player on that side of the board must put one counter in each square from his or her "winnings".
5. The game continues until all the counters have been won, or one player is unable to put the necessary counters down on his or her side of the board.

15

Player 1   Player 2

- *How do you go about teaching someone to play a new game?*

- *How would you expect the text to be set out?*

- *What might you need to think about as we read?*

When reading this text, the teacher may need to stop after every instruction to give the students time to consider the instruction or to carry it out. The text may need to be read a number of times before the students are clear about the rules of the game.

Shared Writing

Dancing with the Pen, Chapter 3, suggests ways of choosing topics that could be appropriate for shared writing and offers ideas about the teacher's role in shared writing.

The shared writing approach helps students develop their understanding of written language. With the teacher's help, students record their own experiences and ideas in their own words. The writing is then published in a variety of forms and made available for all to read.

This approach is used in many classrooms in the early years, especially with students who require extra support to expand and enrich their understanding of written language. Older students can benefit from this approach as both producers and interpreters of the oral and written language.

---

41   J. Hall, "How to play Ô làng," *School Journal,* Part 4 Number 2 (1992): p. 15

Talking, writing, and reading can be based on common school experiences — a trip, a visitor to the classroom, Halloween — as well as on individual experiences with students' friends, family, or interests. Because the talking and writing are products of each student's thoughts about their own world, they have a unique meaning.

Other people's words can also provide a starting point for student and teacher. Written language can be the origin of shared writing as well as the product of it. Students can innovate on the language of a particular book, retelling a story in a new way by keeping to the original structures but inserting new vocabulary. This kind of writing — partly following a model and partly creating something new — can be a useful step towards understanding how written language works and how people can use words.

Students' Own Text and Early Reading

Text that students have produced from their own experience, using familiar language patterns, makes good emergent and early reading material.

The novice reader can anticipate more closely what the text might say if it is written in something like the way that [the child] might say it. [42]

Students' own text, based on their own language, feelings, and thoughts, is often concrete and vivid, with lively language structures and vocabulary that relates directly to their own personal experiences. Sometimes the vocabulary and language structures may be more lively than those found in published readers. For example, from a five-year-old: "I spent my lunch money on Space Invaders, and Jimmy gave me a sandwich, but I was ravenous when I got home."

Reading text that they themselves have written is especially motivating for learner readers.

The texts produced by students contribute to the core of classroom reading material. Their own writing and that of their friends has an irresistible appeal for most students.

Shared Writing with ESL Students

The shared writing approach is especially useful for ESL students because the text reflects the students' own experiences. Depending on the stage the students have reached, the teacher will either write down what students tell or encourage them to do this for themselves.

Reading material produced in this way gives both students and teacher some common background for understanding. The teacher should always show respect for other points of view. The recording of ideas may initially be in the student's first language.

Writers who are new learners of English may need special help in getting their ideas on paper or on the [computer] screen, but like beginning writers, they should be "writing" their own text from the start if possible.

Dancing with the Pen, page 58

It is important for teachers to acknowledge that many students learning English are literate in another language. Their first language strengths should be recognized and built on, because a continued growth in the first language is desirable for optimum development in English.

---

42   Clay, *Becoming Literate: The construction of inner control*, p. 191

Many of the benefits of shared writing remain the same for all students, and learning to read in a second language involves most of the same processes as learning to read in a first language. However, teachers need to note particular difficulties that these students might encounter when reading in English. They should provide support for the students in picking out key words and anticipating what is about to be read on the basis of semantic and syntactic information. Students learning English may not have sufficient knowledge of the background culture, or of the structure of the language, to make accurate predictions using these sources of information.

Shared Writing with Older Fluent Readers

With older students, shared writing continues to be a very valuable teaching approach. The aim is still to extend students' command of written language. At this stage, students can often read and write using more complex structures than normally occur in their spoken language. In fact, as their written language takes on some of the features that they find in texts they are reading, their oral language too may be extended.

The teacher's role with older students is to help them record their experiences and ideas in different ways. For example, instead of encouraging students to recount their experience of making hot air balloons, the teacher could help them write an explanation of how hot air balloons work or a set of instructions for making them.

Students should be introduced to new ways of writing in a shared situation, where they have support. Often, the teacher acts as scribe so that the students can focus their attention on the structure of the text. The questions the teacher asks should guide the students naturally into new ways of writing.

The teacher's main aim in shared writing is to extend students' confidence in communicating through written language.

Guided Reading

Guided reading is the heart of the balanced literacy program. It gives a teacher and a group of students the opportunity to talk, read, and think their way purposefully through a text. It is the approach that helps students become fluent, independent readers.

In shared reading, the teacher reads the text aloud, modeling the processes and strategies necessary to read fluently, but in guided reading, the teacher helps a group of students use these strategies to read a text themselves. The teacher has a critical role in preparing the lesson and in teaching, observing, and supporting each student during guided reading.

Guided reading is an approach that is appropriate at all levels of the school, from emergent readers to the most capable students. In the early stages, guided reading is taken three to five days a week. With older fluent readers, it can be taken less regularly.

Guided reading:

- ensures that students read a new text successfully;

- helps students develop positive attitudes towards reading;

- provides an opportunity for students to develop and practice reading strategies necessary to read independently;

- allows teachers to observe students while they process unfamiliar texts;

- gives teachers and students an opportunity to explore the features of the language used in a variety of texts.

Guided reading is usually taken with small groups of about four to eight students. Groups can be based on students' interests, experiences, and ability, but they need to change from time to time as students develop at different rates and as the teacher identifies the different needs of individual students.

In any guided reading session, the teacher needs to know what knowledge and understandings each child will bring to the reading and what supports or assistance will be necessary to ensure that the students can read the text successfully. Choosing the "right" text is very important. The aim is to choose a text that the students can (with the teacher's guidance) read successfully, but that includes a number of challenges to "stretch" the students a little.

The ultimate goal in guided reading is to teach the students to use reading strategies independently so that they can read new texts successfully and be able to discuss them critically.

Guided reading may be started with children who have developed some understandings about reading. They:

- know that reading makes sense and "sounds right";

- understand the directionality of reading;

- can match the spoken words with each written word;

- can recognize and write a few words, including their name;

- are able to match the same word written in different contexts;

- are learning to use meaning and structural and visual sources of information (see pages 23–25) to figure out unknown words.

A few children develop these understandings quickly and may be ready to begin guided reading early in their first year; others may develop them later.

The key elements of guided reading involve:

- **choosing** an appropriate text;
- **introducing** the text;
- **reading** the text;
- **discussing** the reading;
- **evaluating** the students' reading of the text.

Choosing an Appropriate Text

The texts used for guided reading at the emergent and early stages are usually complete books of up to 16 pages in length. With older fluent readers, short stories, non-fiction pieces, poems, and even chapters from longer books are used.

The teacher selects texts that are:

- at a level where there are enough challenges and supports to allow new learning;
- not familiar to the students;
- interesting and/or informative;
- suitable for practicing a particular strategy;
- appropriate in length — five to ten minutes of independent reading;
- representative of a balance between fiction and non-fiction;
- available in sets so that each child has a copy.

The teacher's aim is always to help students understand what they read. By being helped to develop and use problem-solving strategies, students can learn to solve meaning and word difficulties independently. If the text is too difficult, children are prevented from problem-solving, and the reading process breaks down into meaningless "word calling."

Introducing the Text

The orientation or opening discussion should be short — no longer than five minutes. It usually draws on recent experiences, a topic of interest, the title of the text, the illustrations, author, main characters, place names, or at the emergent level, walking the children through the pictures and/or the pattern of the story. The important thing is that the students know enough about the text to read it successfully.

The teacher and students need to be clear about the purpose or purposes for reading. It is useful to discuss a particular strategy you want the students to focus on, such as using visual information, locating information, using diagrams, or analyzing character development. Some teachers use an easel to write down questions, predictions, or text features, to help students focus during the reading.

Unfamiliar words and concepts should be discussed conversationally before the reading. This discussion provides a context for the reader when the words are encountered later in the text. Some words and concepts may require further clarification during and following the reading.

Note: Some teachers prefer to have the group focus on one book that the teacher holds, rather than giving out individual copies at this stage.

By the time they come to read the text independently, the students should:

- be keen to read the story;

- be clear about the strategy to focus on;

- have made predictions about the text or what they will learn from the text;

- have some knowledge of how to cope with the difficulties they will encounter;

- be familiar with any new structures, unusual vocabulary, or proper names.

Reading the Text

Most books used with young children can be read right through without a break, but in some cases, particularly with older fluent readers, texts can be read in one or two chunks with a brief discussion in the break to improve comprehension. Each student is expected to read silently. Emergent readers are encouraged to read softly to themselves so as not to distract other readers. "Round robin" reading, where each student takes a turn at reading aloud, is not appropriate because it prevents each student from processing the text and constructing meaning independently.

Teachers can use guided reading to help students develop new reading strategies.

During the "silent reading," the teacher "listens in," intervening only where necessary, to help a student with a difficulty. Students are encouraged to use the strategies they have been learning in shared reading to solve any challenges in the text independently. This is a good time to take a running record of a child. Observations taken at this time and recorded on a clipboard are invaluable for preparing for future teaching.

Students gradually take more and more responsibility for their own reading.

For older students, who are reading longer texts, it is useful to prepare one or two questions or tasks on a chart for the fast finishers. This prevents these students from distracting the students still reading.

Discussing the Reading

After all children in the group have finished reading, they can be asked to talk about the text and to ask questions about it. The teacher needs to have prepared questions to facilitate discussion, but students should be encouraged to ask questions, too. It is a good time to return to the predictions they made about the text before they began reading for affirmation. For some texts, it is important to talk about the author's message or debate various points of view, because this sort of conversation helps students "get beneath the surface" of the text.

Talking about the difficulties some of the students had and the strategies used to solve them helps reinforce good reading behavior, particularly for those students who are not confident readers. It is helpful to use an easel to write down and analyze words that have proved difficult or interesting. This is also a good time to examine letter-sound relationships, letter clusters, and parts of words, using the context of the text. The easel can be used to chart such things as the plot, main ideas, facts and opinions, features of text, or technical vocabulary.

The discussion should not go on too long. With emergent readers, it might last up to five minutes, and with older fluent readers, it might last for about ten minutes. The text should be available to the student for a few days so that they can reread it, or in the case of younger readers, take it home to read it to someone else in the family.

What happens after reading will be determined by the nature of the text, the students' responses to it, and the purpose the teacher and students had in mind. Often, the reading is sufficient in itself, particularly if the students have had ample opportunity to discuss experiences, ideas, storyline, characters, or information and to anticipate and confirm their understandings of the text.

The best way for students to become good at reading is to do a great deal of it.

Some related activities after reading may help to extend and enrich the experiences gained during the reading of the text. The best way for students to become good at reading is to do a great deal of it. Most of all, students need many texts that they can read successfully, and the time and opportunity to read them.

Evaluating the Students' Reading of the Text

Guided reading provides a great opportunity to evaluate students' reading development. By observing individual students reading, by taking running records, and by discussing the ways various students solve word difficulties, the teacher can learn a great deal about their reading behavior. If this information is recorded, it can be used for future lessons to help students use effective reading strategies. In this way, a teacher can monitor each student's reading behavior and help them progress through a series of increasingly difficult books.

Guided Reading with Fluent Readers — an Example

In this example of guided reading, the teacher uses *The Belle of the Ball* by Beverley Dunlop.[43] The purpose of the session is to help students consider a range of opinions and justify their point of view by referring back to the text.

Choosing the Text

- The story is easy to read but elicits a wide range of opinions.

- It is short and can be completed in one session.

- The students are likely to have similar personal experiences to bring to the text.

Challenges for the students:

- the title and how this relates to the story;

- the subtle way the author introduces the issue of cultural differences between Beverley and her father.

Introducing the Text

Before introducing the text, the teacher asks the students to discuss their first school dance. This reveals the background experiences the students bring to the story. Students then discuss the title and illustrations, predicting how Beverley feels and how she is reacting to the coming school dance.

Once the students have established that there is a mismatch between the title and the illustrations, provide a focus for reading by asking the following questions:

- *Why does Beverley look so miserable?*

- *Why did the author choose to call the story* The Belle of the Ball?

- *Choose the character you think is most at fault, and think of some advice to give them.*

Reading the Text

In the story, there is a point (turning point or plot point) where things could get better or worse for Beverley. The students read up to this point; then they stop

---

43 *School Journal,* Part 4 Number 1 (1980), pp. 30–32

and decide what they would like to happen if they were Beverley and what they think will happen in the story. They then read silently to the end of the story.

Discussing the Reading

During the discussion, the teacher encourages a range of viewpoints. Students justify their opinions by referring to the text to support their argument. To see if the students pick up the cultural differences between Beverley and her father, the teacher asks why the author mentioned the father was Russian. The students look at features of the dialog to see whether the language exposes the cultural differences.

Students are encouraged to look at what happened in the story through the eyes of various characters.

Follow-up Activity

After reading the story, the students create a semantic web to show the complexities of the relationships between the characters.

Semantic Web

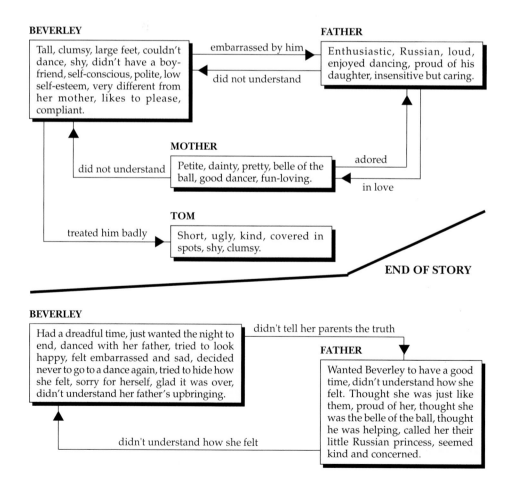

Reciprocal Teaching

A useful technique for fluent readers is known as "reciprocal teaching." This variation on the guided reading approach enables the responsibility for leading the discussion to shift from the teacher to the members of the group in a planned and structured way.[44] Reciprocal teaching is a valuable small-group approach for improving students' comprehension and critical reading. The preparation and organization necessary for reciprocal teaching is basically the same as for guided reading; the main difference is that the students gradually take over more and more responsibility for generating the discussion and critically examining the text. The technique is like a dialog between teacher and students for jointly interpreting a text. It involves the members of the group in making predictions, clarifying ideas, generating questions, and summarizing information.

Class Management for Guided Reading

Guided reading can take place at a table, at a group of desks, or on a rug on the floor. A small circle is the best configuration because each student and the teacher can see each other when reading and discussing the text.

While the teacher takes guided reading with a group, the other students should be involved in purposeful literacy activities.

To enable a teacher to withdraw a small group for uninterrupted guided reading requires managing the class so that everyone is engaged in independent literacy activities. This takes time and student training. It is important to teach routines to the students by modeling the activities to the class several times. For example:

- how to work in small groups;

- how to read with a partner;

- what to do when finished;

- when and how to move to another activity;

- how to use the class library;

- how to move about in the classroom;

- how to maintain acceptable noise levels;

- what to do when needing help.

The purposeful literacy activities suggested below will engage most students for a sustained period of time while the teacher is working with a group for guided reading or holding an individual conference. Some activities are more suitable for younger students.

---

44 Two useful articles about reciprocal teaching are: A. S. Palincsar and A. L. Brown, "Reciprocal Teaching of Comprehension-fostering and Comprehension-monitoring Activities," *Cognition and Instruction*, vol. 1 (1984): pp. 117–175; and Marie Kelly and Dennis Moore, "I've Found My Memory! Reciprocal teaching in a primary school," *SET* 2 (1993): item 8, pp. 1–4

Independent Reading

This is the most important and valuable activity. Students can read silently at tables, on the rug, or in the class library. A large number of suitable fiction and non-fiction texts that students can read independently should be available. Monitoring by the teacher will ensure that students are choosing appropriate materials and are reading them successfully.

Play Reading

A small group of students reads a play silently and then chooses parts to read aloud. The play could be performed later in front of the class. This activity is best done in a corner of the classroom, or in the corridor, if this is possible.

Audio Center

A small group of students meets at the listening center with books and a tape chosen by the teacher. Students listen to the tape and then follow the text on a second reading. Afterwards, students should read the book independently.

Partner Reading

Students read to each other quietly in pairs, taking turns to read a page. At the end of the reading, each student asks a question about the book, and they discuss it.

Directed Reading

Students are given a non-fiction text that they can read successfully. Written instructions provided give clear directions on what to do with the information in the text and on ways that students can present what they have learned to the class.

Following Instructions

Students are given a list of instructions that they have to follow exactly. When they have completed the task, they present the finished product to the class.

Arranging Sentence Strips in Pockets

Students practice reading, matching, and sequencing sentence strips on familiar poems, rhymes, news stories, class stories, recipes, big books, songs, and so on.

Alphabet and Spelling Games

Students play alphabet games of various kinds, including magnetic letters and jigsaw letters, and related games such as bingo games, memory games, crossword puzzles, and snap games, with words needing revision.

Most teachers take guided reading in the morning during a large block of uninterrupted time (usually ninety minutes). To allow teachers, particularly of young students, to reach one or two groups for guided reading and to monitor independent activities each day requires setting up a rotation system that children can follow easily. For further suggestions, see Chapter 7, Organizing for Reading.

Independent Reading

Independent reading is central to successful reading development. To become lifelong readers, students need to choose to read, select their own material, and share what they have read. Teachers need to encourage independent reading at every stage of students' reading development. Independent reading should be integral to the daily program in every classroom.

Key elements of independent reading are:

- choosing texts;

- space and time for reading;

- responding to texts;

- conferencing with students;

- time for instruction.

Choosing Texts

The teacher has an important role in providing texts for students at the emergent and early stages of reading development. When students have access to a wide range of reading material, they can practice their fledgling reading strategies on familiar, and occasionally non-familiar, material. The texts provided in the class library and book baskets should reflect a balance between familiar favorites and new material, and between fiction and non-fiction.

Emergent and early readers should also have access to poems, songs, chants, rhymes, stories, big books, and student writing that has been previously shared by the teacher. These texts will all be familiar to the students and provide a rich resource for independent reading. Establishing individual or group reading baskets in the classroom ensures a ready supply of easy texts for beginning readers. Books in the baskets should include those already used in shared and guided reading. The students should have a role in selecting these texts, which should be changed regularly.

For younger fluent readers, a good variety of easy chapter books and longer picture books should be available. A variety of interesting non-fiction is essential. For fluent readers taking responsibility for selecting their own books from the class, school, and community library, the teacher's role changes. As well as providing a range of texts, the teacher now provides information about a range of sources of texts. As members of a community of readers, however, teachers and students will continue to share information about particular texts that they have enjoyed or found useful.

Space and Time to Read

Students should have opportunities to read independently every day. For many students, sitting still and reading quietly has to be learned. To begin with, students may be able to sustain only ten to fifteen minutes' reading, but with practice this can be extended to over thirty minutes, even in the early years.

A comfortable book corner in the classroom with a rug and cushions is an ideal place to read. It should be in a well-lit, comfortable, easily accessible part of the room, and not in the path of the main traffic flow, where students would be frequently distracted or disturbed. However, reading at desks and tables is appropriate in many classrooms.

Responding to Texts

If students are to enjoy and understand literary and expository texts to the full, they need to have opportunities to talk and write about them. Talking in small groups of four to six students about a short story, picture book, article, or novel is a valuable way for students to clarify the ideas or understandings of the text. For this book talk to be successful, it must be modeled in class discussions following a read-aloud session or during shared or guided reading.

Written responses, in the form of short letters to other students and/or the teacher, help students to share and clarify ideas about the books they are reading. Journal or diary entries can also be used. Nancie Atwell found that amongst adolescents, "written responses to books would go deeper than their talk, that writing would give them time to consider their thinking and their thoughts captured would spark new insights."[45]

Drawing favorite or exciting scenes is a response that many students enjoy and learn from. Visual and oral presentations can be encouraged when several students have read the same book.

Conferencing with Students

While students are involved in independent reading, the teacher needs to monitor their levels of interest, their understanding of what they read, and the

---

45 Nancie Atwell, *In the Middle, Writing, Reading and Learning with Adolescents* (Portsmouth, New Hampshire: Heinemann, 1987)

amount of reading they do. This can be done by small-group or individual conferences or by observing the independent reading behavior of the class as a whole. The insights gained are used to plan further teaching. Teachers can use independent reading sessions to develop areas of learning and extend students' ranges of reading in these areas. They may select books by author, genre, or content-area study.

Students read independently as they search for information to use in a piece of their own written work. Teachers can stimulate students' interests by recommending suitable, relevant books and reading short extracts. Students should also be given the opportunity to promote books to others.

It is very important that the teacher discusses and monitors what students are doing when they choose and read books by themselves. Conferences should be a regular part of independent reading.

Some understandings and behaviors that can be monitored during independent reading:

- what books students are reading (see example of reading log);

- how long students can sit and read quietly;

- strategies and sources of information that students are using to solve meaning and word difficulties;

- other times that students read;

- who the students talk or write to about books;

- how the students know they have made a good choice;

- how students choose books;

- what students do when they are reading a book that is too hard;

- who are their favorite authors.

As well as these, note all the features of the text that students can learn and talk about in Chapter 6, Responding to Texts.

Independent reading sessions provide valuable opportunities for teachers to gain insights into their students' reading behavior.

Respond to Independent-read Texts
1.

READING LOG

Title	Author	Pages	Date started	Date finished	Rating
Charlotte's Web	E. B. White	175	Jan 7	Jan 12	9/10
The House at Pooh Corner	A. A. Milne	176	Jan 14	Jan 19	8/10
Frog and Toad are Friends	Arnold Lobel	62	Feb 3	Feb 3	6/10
New Year Festivals	Sheila Hatherley	30	Feb 7	Feb 8	7/10

Time for Instruction

It is worth using a few minutes during independent reading to take a minilesson with the class or whole group on such things as:

- writing a book review;

- always carrying a book to read;

- using removable adhesive stickers to mark points of interest, confusion, ideas to discuss with other students;

- writing responses to other students or the teacher;

- making a schedule of the times when independent reading can be fitted in at home and at school;

- looking at theme and its relation to plot or at point of view in an article.

Teachers who love books and reading will find it easy to create a community of readers within the classroom. In this community, students and the teacher will want to talk about the books they are reading and will not be afraid to ask questions or seek clarification about something in a book. Students will read to and with each other, helping less able students, and will always be making recommendations to others about books.

Choosing Reading Materials

Teachers need to make informed choices about the texts they use for shared and guided reading, the books they read aloud to the class, and the resources they provide in the classroom for independent reading. Reading materials should meet the varied abilities and interests of the students.

All teachers should read widely, have a sound knowledge of quality children's literature, and keep up to date with recent publications. This task is both important and highly enjoyable.

When choosing books to read aloud, teachers should include a range of styles and genres so that students have access to many models to use in their own reading and writing.

Criteria for Text Selection

The texts used for reading should be the best available. They should be meaningful and memorable texts that excite and inform students and help them understand themselves and the world. Such texts convince students that reading is worthwhile and satisfying so that it becomes an important part of their lives. When selecting reading material from the wide range available, teachers may find it helpful to ask themselves the following questions:

Teachers can make informed choices about texts for their students by applying criteria such as those set out below.

General

Is the text attractive?

Do the illustrations complement the writing?

Are the typeface and layout clear?

Fiction

Will the story appeal?

Is the story worth reading?

Does the story avoid stereotyping?

Are the characters believable?

Do the illustrations, the typeface, and the layout make the text more meaningful?

Does the story live up to the expectations raised by its title and cover?

Is the language appropriate? Is the shape of the story satisfying?

Will the story stand being read repeatedly? (Not all stories need to be.)

Non-fiction

Does the writer understand the subject?

Is the information accurate?

Is the text up to date?

Does the writer avoid talking down to the reader?

Is the language straightforward and meaningful?

Is specialized vocabulary made understandable?

Do the illustrations, maps, graphs, or diagrams support the text? Are they well labeled?

Does the text have an index, a glossary, a table of contents?

Matching Students with Suitable Texts

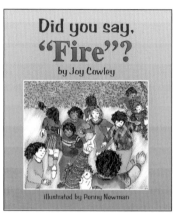

When choosing texts for students, consider the content as well as the level. Students who are really interested in the content of a text will put more into reading it and get more out of it.

Some publishers suggest "reading levels" for their materials, but teachers need to confirm or amend such recommendations on the basis of their knowledge of their own students. The difficulty level of the vocabulary is important, but other factors also affect readability. These include the syntactic complexity of the text, the number of abstract or complex ideas it presents, its physical layout, and the illustrations. (Note that the levels given to the books used in Reading Recovery are not designed to be used with students in regular classroom programs.)

Look through a text to decide which of its features will meet your students' learning needs. For example, a teacher using the book *Did you say, "Fire"?*[46] might consider the following features:

- the strong storyline with its identifiable beginning, middle, and ending;

- the repetitive structure throughout most of the story;

- the changes in print size (between the text in boxes and in the illustrations);

- the length of many of the sentences;

- the combination of book language and natural language;

- the match between illustrations and print, which varies from simple (as in the middle picture) to complex (as in the lower picture);

- the way the printed book provides opportunities for developing understanding through using the letter-sound associations of initial letters and endings within the same page, for example, *sniffed* and *squeaked,* or *fire* and *fighters.*

---

46 Joy Cowley, *Did you say, "Fire"?* Guided Reading series (Wellington: Learning Media Limited, 1997)

Supports and Challenges for Students

The teacher needs to consider carefully how many features of a chosen text will be challenges and how many will be supports for a particular student or group of students. Ask yourself these questions:

Do the language (or languages), experiences, and expectations that the student brings to the reading match those in the text?

Will the text connect with the student's culture?

Is the student familiar with the type of language used? How complex are the vocabulary and syntax?

Are the concepts at an appropriate level of understanding for the student? How abstract are the ideas? How complex are they? Is the writing that presents them simple or dense?

Does the student have the appropriate reading strategies for this text?

Is the student likely to be interested in the content? Will all students be reading the text?

Will the layout, graphics, and illustrations enhance the student's response to and understanding of the text?

Is the text suitable for guided, shared, or independent reading? What is the purpose for using the text?

Knowledge of the students from running records, and observation of the students, form the basis for decision-making.

6 Responding to Texts

Looking Further into Texts

Students should be encouraged to read widely, analyze and evaluate written texts, and develop their ability to make meaning out of increasingly challenging text. They should think critically about what they read, and understand that written language varies according to context.[47]

Readers respond to texts in a variety of ways. Their initial responses are usually intuitive and personal. By encouraging students to read closely and look further into texts, teachers can extend students' vocabularies, increase their understanding of the effects of words, language features, and techniques, and help them think critically about language and meaning. Such understanding will enhance and enrich students' personal reading.

It is not necessary to search all texts for deeper meanings. Many work very well on the surface level, for example, recipes, instructions, or how to play a game. Helping readers look further into a text should never invalidate their initial experience of reading it. Students should be able to enjoy a story, a poem, a description, or an article for its own sake and respond to it naturally.

There are three important questions that teachers should ask. Some come before a detailed study, some after. They are:

- *What do you think this text is about?*

- *Why do you think it was written, and who for?*

And, most importantly,

- *What is **your** reaction to it? Do you understand or like what it's saying?*

In this chapter, a variety of genres is discussed. Teachers can find more information on the features of different kinds of text, for example, in B. Derewianka's book *Exploring How Texts Work,*[48] which also includes teaching suggestions.

Texts can contain several levels of meaning. In narrative texts, the "story behind the story" can be found as readers come to understand the motivation of the characters, the force and shape of the storyline, the way the setting is presented, and the ways language is used. Readers often need to look beneath the surface of the narrative, drama, or poem to discover the statements the work is making about human life. Words and ideas in literary texts are open to different interpretations and require readers to use their imagination.

Like narrative texts, expository texts contain statements about human life and are often in the form of explanations and analyses. These texts relate to proven facts, received standards of measurement or classification, and theories or opinions that are validated in some scientific or practical way.

In expository texts, readers expect to discover a more precise meaning in the words. The deeper level of understanding lies in the readers' perception

Helping readers look further into a text should never invalidate their initial experience in reading it.

---

47 *English in the New Zealand Curriculum,* p. 33
48 B. Derewianka, *Exploring How Texts Work* (Rozelle, NSW: Primary English Teaching Association, 1990)

97

of accuracy or bias, their accumulation of knowledge, or their appreciation of the clarity of the text. Appreciative understanding of a good expository text may lead readers to take more efficient action, to change their actions, or to make a sharper analysis of the world around them.

A Wide Range of Reading Experiences

We read for many purposes: for enjoyment and relaxation, to find out about people and places, to study information, to follow directions, and to learn how to construct things. The texts that we read include both fiction and factual texts in varied forms and genres. Note that the same genres can be used to fulfill different functions and that the same strategies are common to many reading tasks.

We read a wide range of texts for independent and critical reading, for pleasure and information.

In the following pages, several different types of text are explored. Some questions and activities to assist critical reading are suggested. The questions and activities have been arranged under the headings Thinking Critically, Exploring Language, and Processing Information. None of these understandings and behaviors should be considered in isolation. Refer to pages 50–53.

Exploring and learning about the language of a variety of texts increases students' awareness of how language varies over time and according to context. This knowledge will help them respond confidently to, and develop control over, the wide range of texts and language uses required for learning and living in society.[49]

---

49 *English in the New Zealand Curriculum*, p. 17

Narrative Texts

Reading and telling stories to children, and sharing storybooks with them, are natural ways of getting them hooked on reading. Like adults, children enjoy the experience of being lost in a good narrative.

Think of the anticipation of reading an exciting or moving story, the sense of wonder, the feeling of identification with certain characters, the shiver of excitement or suspense, the laughter or tears, the regret when the book comes to an end. In this type of reading, the reader relates closely to the story and gets inside it, living through the events with the characters. This involves exploration. The reader roams around inside the story "trying on roles, predicting outcomes, even retreating when necessary."[50] The author seeks to create levels beneath the surface meaning of the text and engages readers in a dialogue as they fill out meanings with their own emotions and experiences. Narrative texts provide a source of vicarious experience that can "fire the imagination with sensory and emotive images to provoke imagined experience."[51] This type of reading arouses our senses and emotions, gives richness to our language, and adds to our store of understanding.

Most narrative texts can be discussed in terms of the features shown in the table on page 100. For simplicity, these features are looked at separately, but in actual discussion, they should always be related to each other.

It is helpful to discuss narrative texts in terms of the features of the genre — plot, characters, setting, and theme.

---

50 M. Saxby, "The Gift of Wings: The value of literature to children," *Give Them Wings: The experience of children's literature* (South Melbourne: Macmillan, 1987), p. 6
51 M. Saxby, *"The Gift of Wings,"* p. 6

Features	Characteristics	Students should be learning to:
Plot	Sequences of action Plots include introduction, problem, climax or crisis, resolution, and conclusion.	understand how narratives begin, develop, and end; understand the point of view; retell the story; see how the plot is affected by the characters.
Characters	People, animals, and imaginary characters in a narrative Readers can usually identify with one or more and relate the characters' experiences in the story to their personal experiences.	name and define major and minor characters; describe the ways they talk, act, and move, saying what they care for and what they fear; explore how the characters are conveyed; explain how the personalities of the characters affect the plot.
Setting	Places or situations where narrative takes place Setting can have a powerful effect on the theme in the narrative and on the reader's emotions.	describe setting, using a list of adjectives; understand the relationship of the setting to the plot, theme, and character development; understand how setting is conveyed; appreciate the importance of setting in their own writing.
Theme	The subject or message the writer is attempting to communicate Themes can be conveyed in an obvious way or "between the lines."	recognize the author's message; relate the theme of the story to their own beliefs and culture; compare themes from different books; discuss themes in their own writing.

I'M THE KING OF THE MOUNTAIN

by Joy Cowley

illustrated by Dick Frizzell

Plot

Plots, or storylines, are sequences of action. In the course of reading to students or in shared and guided reading, teachers can help students understand how a story develops. The "classic" form of narrative referred to in this section includes: introduction/beginning/setting; problem/development; climax/crisis; resolution/anticlimax; conclusion. The form is not exactly the same in all books or in all cultures.

The Teacher's Role

Children like to read stories with plenty of action. Their own writing will improve, and their enjoyment of reading and writing will increase, as they discover how a good narrative is shaped. However, in creating their own stories, they often need help to develop an effective structure.

While reading a narrative text, students can be helped to appreciate plots and storylines through the following suggested questions and activities.

Thinking Critically

What do you think the story is going to be about?
Share the text and first responses to it. Discuss each other's opinions.
Do you think the story could have happened in real life?
Where do you think the author got the idea for the story from?
Brainstorm the author's idea for the story.
Relate the events of the story to its other aspects, such as character, theme, and setting, explaining the links.
How did you feel at the end of the story? Why?
Say how satisfactory the beginning, development, climax, resolution, and ending of the story are, and give reasons for these judgments.
Did the pictures help you to understand the plot? How? What kinds of illustration are used? Photos? Line drawings? Cartoons? Paintings? Has the illustrator left things out or included things the author did not mention?
Make up a brief for the illustration of this story.

Exploring Language

What bit of the story do you like best? Why? Were some parts of the story more important, or more exciting, or less clear than others? Which were they?
Discuss any parts that are interesting or lively or that drag or seem slow.
Could you tell when something important was about to happen in the story? If so, how?
Discuss any special features that contribute to the plot structure, for example, chapter headings, link sentences, or climaxes.

Building a Language for Discussion

To discuss plots and storylines satisfactorily, students need to build up a vocabulary of terms. These should be introduced in context as the need arises (which might be before, during, or after reading).

Here are some examples of terms relating to text:

- retell, recount, main events, situation, action, interaction, plot, subplot, flashback, introduction, climax, problem, crisis, solution, resolution, anticlimax, conclusion, chapter, paragraph, episode, section, sequence, dialogue, pace, structure …

- action-packed, fast, slow, leisurely, even, jerky, tight, loose …

- good, clear, consistent, sharp …

- ambiguous, vague, simple, obvious, complex, dense …

- poor, muddled, puzzling, contradictory, inconsistent, hard to understand …

Terms like the following can be used of illustrations:

- realistic, accurate, unsuitable, appropriate, stereotyped, detailed, sketchy, imaginative, impressionistic, powerful, emotional, exciting, surrealistic, fantastic, dull, bland, boring.

Processing Information

Identify the main parts of the storyline and create a flow diagram of the action. Select and show main plots, and subplots where necessary.
Does the story jump about in time? (Did it flash forward or flash back?) Where did the climax occur, and what happened afterwards?
Retell, in order, the main things that happened in the story.
Does this author always end stories in the same way?
Collect the opening and closing sentences of different stories and compare their effectiveness.
Recount the main events of the story.
Create a "text" for a wordless book.
Read and discuss each other's writing.
Create narrative by role-playing, adapting, or telling about "missing" parts of the action (including writing an alternative ending).

Here is a teacher's account of helping her students to think critically about the plot in a picture book.

A Teacher's Account of Using a Narrative

I chose *All the King's Horses,* by Michael Foreman, to read aloud to the class as it is a delightful modern fairy tale and has an unexpected ending. Before reading the book together, we discussed fairy tales we were already familiar with, including some of the better known tales about princesses, such as *Cinderella, The Frog Prince,* and *Sleeping Beauty.* We talked about the endings of these stories and why they were usually happy. We discussed similarities in the plots of the traditional fairy tales we had read previously.

While reading the story, I stopped to discuss with the students what the dilemma was that the author had created. I then asked them to predict the outcome. Later, we discussed whether the woodcutter's son would succeed. After finishing reading the story and enjoying the students' reactions, we talked about the similarities and differences between this plot and those of traditional fairy tales. We debated whether the problem in the story had been resolved, and how satisfactory the ending was. The students had a lot of questions and expressed many different opinions.

In groups, some students developed a flow chart to show the sequences of action in the plot. Others created a chart to show the high and low points of the story and where the climax occurred. Then we came back together as a class to share what we had found. Finally, we looked at one another's writing of narratives to see if we could identify the plot clearly.

Flow diagram of <u>All the King's Horses</u>

Princess loves riding horses
↓
King wants her married
↓
King sends out couriers to find husbands
↓
Princess wrestles with them and wins
↓
King extends the search
↓
Woodcutter tries his luck
↓
Woodcutter loses
↓
Princess rides off with all the horses

Characters

Identifying with the characters in a story is one of the ways that people come to terms with their own experiences of life. It is important that the students read narrative to explore the motivations for human action in the light of their own concerns and values. Readers are helped to understand a character's action without necessarily condoning it, and to judge how well the character is developed in, and justified by, the story.

The Teacher's Role

It is not easy for younger readers to describe characters objectively, because they have to distance themselves from those they may have identified with. During discussions and conferences about their judgments, teachers should try to model how to be objective.

While reading a narrative text, students are helped to look further into the characters by the following suggested activities and questions.

Thinking Critically

Describe a friend or family member to others so that they can predict who it might be.

What do you think the characters in this book are going to be like?

Describe characters from any other books or stories you have read by the same author.

What do you know about people like this? (Work habits? Culture? Other things?)

Share a story in which you like or dislike certain characters.

Have you ever met people like the characters in this story?

Consider how fair it is to judge a person by the way they look or speak.

Can you think of a time when you have acted like the characters in this story? Why? How?

How does the action of the character(s) affect the plot?

How do the characters relate to each other?

Draw a sociogram showing how one character relates to others.

How do the characters change during the story? Why do they change?

Do you think the characters dealt well or badly with the problems in the story? How would you have dealt with them?

Did any of the characters behave unexpectedly? What was unexpected, and why didn't you expect it?

Were there characters you couldn't believe in? In what ways were they unbelievable?

Consider how well the characters are described in different books by the same author, or other authors.

Sociogram

How well do you think the illustrations depict the characters? What sort of illustrations are used? Would you have illustrated them differently? How?

Exploring Language

What viewpoint is the story written from (that is, in the first, second, or third person)? How does the author let you know this? Why do you think the author chose to write the story from that point of view ?
How does the language help us to learn about the characters?

Building a Language for Discussion

Help the students build up a vocabulary to describe character, behavior, appearance, and personality. Use terms that arise during class discussions and others from the descriptions in the text. Include words such as:

- main/minor characters …
- hero, antihero, heroine …
- actions, events …
- characterization, role …
- male, female …
- dialogue, conversation …
- facial features …
- general appearance, manner …
- voice and way of speaking, physique …
- way of moving …
- culture and values …

Processing Information

Using sections from the text, build up a picture of what the character is like — in appearance, personality, behavior, occupation, and so on. For example:

> *Upstairs, his grandfather hammered at something — he was always painting, hammering, replacing boards; getting ready, he said, for when good times came back. "And when will that be, Harry?" Grandma asked. "When pigs can fly?" "There's no harm," he said, "no harm …" but never got further than that. He went away with a hurt look on his face, but soon took up his hammering again.[52]*

How does the character talk?
Read out part of a character's conversation that is typical.

Students can be asked to describe the characters from a story in words, pictures, and role-play. They may like to play "character" games — for example, one student chooses one of the characters but does not give the name (other players can search the text for clues). The "character" answers questions about their likes and dislikes, and other students work out which character they are impersonating.

WANTED A PIRATE FOR A JOB

MUST BE ABLE TO…….
1. Drink lots of rum.
2. F.I.G.H.T.
3. Swim in the water with sharks.
4. Read maps.
5. shoot cannons in the right direction.
6. can dig fast for gold.
7. Survive on islands for months at a time.

8. If you think you can be a darn good pirate wait on wrecked beach on November 27.

---

52 Maurice Gee, *The Fat Man* (Auckland: Viking, 1994) p. 50

Setting

The alien, mysterious places in Madeleine L'Engle's *A Swiftly Tilting Planet*, the farm landscape of *Charlotte's Web*, the freezing and isolated landscape of *Julie of the Wolves* by Jean Craighead George, the department store in Don Freeman's *Corduroy*, and the dark wintry forest in *Hansel and Gretel* are all effective settings. The setting of a story often has a powerful effect on the reader's emotions and may tie in with the theme of the story.

The Teacher's Role

Students are often keener to get on with the story than to read descriptions of the places in which the events occur. They often do not realize the effect that setting can have on their enjoyment of the story. But even in a story as simple as *Rosie's Walk* by Pat Hutchins, the farmyard is more than incidental. Its bright workaday area is full of traps for the would-be cunning outsider, the fox. Rosie, who lives in it, is sublimely unaware of the hidden dangers.

While reading a narrative text, students are helped to understand the importance of setting through the following suggested questions and activities.

Thinking Critically

Stimulate the students' ideas about settings by exposing them to pictures, smells, tactile objects, and music and other sounds, as well as text. Discuss memorable places or scenes from the lives of the children themselves or from the lives of their families or friends (possibly using family snapshots). Discuss memorable places in favorite stories. For example:

> *We always camped up at the lake after Christmas. Dad worked in the bush up there, when he was young.*
> *We'd drive up, towing the boat, up the dusty road beside the winding river. I loved it, Mum hated it, and Emma got carsick.*[53]

Have you ever been to a place like the one described in the story? How did you feel about it?

How does the author establish the setting? Does the setting change? Where? How? Why? What mood is created when the change occurs?

Can you imagine this plot in a different setting? What is the effect of the setting on the plot? On the characters?

Does the setting have a deeper level of meaning (metaphorical or symbolic) in the lives of the characters?

Ask students what they notice, in the opening paragraphs, about:

- the place;

- the time of day, period, weather, and season;

- the characters involved;

---

53   Jack Lasenby, *The Lake* (Auckland: Oxford University Press, 1987), p. 1

- the atmosphere, tone, and mood of the story;

- the writer's style and the pace of the language.

(These aspects of the story will probably alter subsequently as the action shifts.)

Exploring Language

Ask the students to look at the illustrations, check the opening sentences or paragraph for special words or phrases, and predict the setting of the story. Later, they could discuss how language is used to convey the setting.

Building a Language for Discussion

The vocabulary that readers need to help them discuss setting are both concrete and emotive. Emotive descriptions of nature include, for example, "the pitiless sea" or "the parched desert." Students can look for emotive terms in passages like this:

> *It was a cruel summer. The heat hadn't let up. The fields were scorched by the sun, the ditches burnt to the dry earth. Under the unrelenting sun, the riverbed cracked like the hide of an old crocodile.*[54]

> *I really loved living in that gipsy caravan. I loved it especially in the evenings … The paraffin lamp was turned low and I could see lumps of wood glowing red-hot in the old stove and wonderful it was to be lying there snug and warm in my bunk in that little room.*[55]

Words that help describe and discuss the setting include:

- country, rural, town, city …   • sea, lake, forest …

- day, night, weather …   • dark, sombre, bright, cheerful …

and also words relating to seasons, shapes, sounds, textures, feelings, and the names of colors.

Processing Information

Where does the story take place? What does the place look/sound/feel like?
Draw a picture, map, or sketch of the setting(s).
Discuss what this story would be like if it happened in a very different place. Would it work as well?
Try the story out in a different setting and see what happens. Has it collapsed?
In *The Silent One* by Joy Cowley (Christchurch, NZ: Whitcoulls, 1981), the setting of a solitary, dumb creature in a deep ocean is important to the story because it symbolizes the boy's predicament. Search for connections of this kind between a particular setting and the characters or the action.
Compare settings in different stories (or settings by different authors), looking for connections between the setting and other features of the story.

---

54   Christiane Moodie, "The Mirage," *School Journal*, Part 4 Number 2 (1990)
55   Roald Dahl, *Danny the Champion of the World* (London: Jonathan Cape, 1975), p. 14

Theme

Authors write in characteristic ways about things that concern them (their themes). A children's author will write about significant issues in a way, and at a level, that children can relate to. Many stories carry particular meanings that may need to be teased out. For example, there is the underlying theme of searching for belonging in Jerry Spinelli's *Maniac Magee*, a message about sibling rivalry in *Julius, the Baby of the World* by Kevin Henkes, and a focus on love and death in Katherine Paterson's *Bridge to Terabithia*.

The Teacher's Role

When considering the author's theme, students are encouraged to find out more about the author, or to write to the author, expressing their views or seeking more information. Before, during, and after reading, students are helped to understand the author's theme through the following questions and activities.

Thinking Critically

What is a theme?
Think about some of the stories read recently, and identify the theme.
Brainstorm ideas on issues that come up in a particular story.
Can you identify with the themes presented in this story? Is this story trying to tell us something about people and the way they live? If so, what is it?
What do you think is the main theme of the story? Explain why you think so.
Write a sentence describing an ideal that the author believes in or values. Do you agree with the author about this ideal?
Have you ever read another story that is trying to say the same kinds of things? If so, tell how it was done in that story. Why do you think these ideas are being presented in this book?

Exploring Language

Discuss any special features of language that help to convey the theme or themes (for example, symbolism or repetition).

Building a Language for Discussion

Words and phrases that describe general ideas and themes include:

* growing up, jealousy, fear, making friends, failure, success, younger or older brothers or sisters, leaving home, adventure, romance, danger, traveling, parent trouble, playing tricks, losing or getting pets …

* injustice, prejudice, snobbery, power, sports, outdoors, death, love, relationships, courage, fear, family, superficial, caring, selfish …

- topic, subject, goal, idea, concept, theme, message, issue, values, beliefs, attitude …

- romantic, realistic, historical, urban, rural …

Processing Information

Students can make use of favorite authors' themes in their own writing or discuss how illustrations relate to the theme. Illustration often plays an important part in establishing the theme, especially in picture books.

Plays

Most of us enjoy watching plays and taking part in them. Getting inside the storyline, trying on the roles, analyzing structure, looking at character development, and considering the appropriateness and effectiveness of dialogue are all part of reading and acting a play.

Features	Students should be learning to:
Plays, like narrative texts, include plots, characters, settings, and themes. Plays are texts written to be acted. In the classroom setting, plays are often read aloud by students, who take the parts of various characters in the play.	enjoy reading and acting plays; discuss the ways the writer creates the setting or staging and exploits the dramatic possibilities of dialogue; understand the conventions of drama texts, including ways of differentiating the characters; identify plot, acts, and scenes; read aloud in a way that suits a particular character.

Action is very important to children, and their humor often lies in slapstick. Slapstick plays are some of the most popular texts. At times, teachers may fall back on reading a play simply because they know that the students will enjoy it. But plays have more to offer than this. They can enhance students' purposeful enjoyment of reading in a particular way because they combine all the forms of language — written, spoken, visual, and body language. In our literate society, we still have great need for articulate and sincere speakers. Reading and acting plays develops the potential actor's or public speaker's sense of presence, and the ability to give others an articulate response. It provides students with practice in oral reading.

When students know that they are going to act in a play, they are likely to read the text more intensively than usual, imagining the characters, exploring their own interpretations, speaking the words, "living" the action. They move from a private experience to a shared one.

The Teacher's Role

Before, during, and after reading, students are helped to look further into the features of plays through the following activities and questions.

Thinking Critically

Discuss relevant past experiences with plays. Talk about how a particular play's dialogue and stage directions are laid out. Discuss its characters, action, dramatic effects, and presentation. Share your favorite part of the play by reading, acting out, or talking.

What do you think the play is about?

What are the play's underlying problems or conflicts? How are they resolved?

Who are the main characters? What are they like? How are they made to seem real?

How do the characters relate to each other?
Take a story and divide it into "acts" and "scenes".
What effect does the play's division into acts and scenes have on how it is read and acted?
Is the meaning of the play better understood when it is acted? If so, why?

Exploring Language

Discuss the main differences between reading a play and a story. Explore some of the dialogue in a play, and discuss the different ways characters can be presented on the stage.

Building a Language for Discussion

Teachers and students may like to use the following words to describe and discuss plays:

- play, drama, skit, revue, playwright, writer, reviewer, action, character, dialogue, prompt …

- act, scene, prologue, epilogue, applause …

- actor, star, cast, supporting actor, role, part, director, producer, designer, stage manager, stagehand, stage directions, exit, enter, performance, critic, review, theater, stalls, circle, box, gallery, spotlight, footlights, box office …

Processing Information

Which character in the play would you like to act, and why?
Prepare and give a play reading.
What would you do differently if you acted the play again?
How is the text structured (in terms of scenes and acts)?
Where is the climax? How can you tell?
Try doing the play in a very different setting.
What happens to the storyline, the characters, and the dialogue?
Adapt a favorite story or school experience into a play.

Poetry

Some poems tell a story, and share the characteristics of stories in narrative and dramatic form. Other kinds of poetry may express one very simple idea or mood.

Features	Students should be learning to:
Ideas are usually expressed in metrical or rhythmic form. Forms include rhymes, ballads, sonnets, free verse, jingles, and haiku.	enjoy listening to and reading poetry; appreciate sound, rhyme, rhythm, and meaning in poetry; explore deeper levels of meaning in imagery and metaphor; discuss conventions used in poetry and how the language relates to the subject; speak poetry aloud from memory, individually and chorally.

From their earliest days, children absorb the rhythms and sounds of their language. From babyhood, this language is extended by nursery rhymes, songs, and word games.

Children often enjoy humorous, light-hearted verse, magic, fantasy, and story poems. These are as much a part of poetic experience as more serious verse. In the best poetry, form and message interact. The first things to enjoy in poetry are sound and meaning. These often speak to the reader on an emotional level, and an intellectual analysis of them does not always increase the reader's enjoyment of the poem and empathy with it.

Little blue eyes
Little white socks
Long tail,
Like a bit of string.

—Mark.

The Teacher's Role

The poem's message and the feelings it evokes are important, but one should not "do a poem to death." It is more important for students to read and enjoy poetry and write their own poems than to analyze poetic forms and meters. Reading or listening to good poetry read with understanding and enthusiasm enables students to build up their awareness of what language can do — and to appreciate the different forms of poetry. Their ability to respond to poetry can be exploited successfully even at the emergent stage of reading.

Before, during, and after reading, students can be helped to look further into the meaning and features of poetry through the following activities and questions.

Thinking Critically

Introduce suitable poets, and discuss any of their poems that the students have read. Read poems you enjoy, and talk about them. Find out what the students think a poem looks like and is. If possible, all their ideas should be accepted.

Discuss the title of a particular poem, and ask the students to predict what the poem is about. When appropriate, brainstorm sensory ideas (pictures, smells, sounds, actions, and so on) that relate to the subject of the poem.

Read poems aloud, and ask yourself:

- *What do you think this poem is about?*

- *How does the poet make comparisons? (similes and metaphors)*

- *Does the poem change the way you think about something? If so, how?*

How does the way the thoughts are expressed differ in these two examples?

The road was a ribbon of moonlight Over the purple moor.	The moon lit up the narrow road winding through the heather on the moor.

Exploring Language

Look at individual words and lines, and ask yourself:

- *What word rhymes with this one?*

- *What line or phrase has the same beat as this one?*

- *What stanza has the same pattern as this one?*

- *Can you find any examples of metaphor and other images? What impact do they have?*

Compare the ways in which different poets treat the same topic.

Building a Language for Discussion

Teachers will need to note words that are especially relevant to their current objectives relating to poetry. These words could be ones that will help students to describe and discuss the form and style of poems.

- rhyme, rhythm, sound, sweet, harsh, soft, loud, hissing, banging …

- verse, pattern, pace, regular, uneven, syncopated, jumpy, beat, strong, weak …

- like, similar, unlike, different, synonym, antonym, opposite …

- word, phrase, noun, adjective, verb, adverb, image, simile, metaphor …

Processing Information

What are your favorite poems? Why do you like them?
Make a class anthology of poetry by selecting class favorites.
Which poem would you like to read again? What bits do you like especially? Why?
What are the most unusual or interesting or the funniest or most exciting words or phrases? How many of the words you chose are adjectives or verbs?
Write your own poetry.

A teacher describes how she used a poem with a group of able readers aged eleven to twelve. The poem[56] has an irregular rhyming pattern and imagery.

A Teacher's Account of Using a Poem with Fluent Readers

Weird Fish

I like to catch the weird fish
with legs and pop-eyes
that live in our creek:
"crawlies", we call them.
I cooked some once —
they tasted like mud.
One day I met this girl
(she was standing in the creek
with her jeans rolled up).
She said, "I know your brother."
I said, "Do you mean the one
who hates girls
and breeds katipo spiders:
or the one who tells old ladies
he's heard on the news
all the tigers have escaped from a circus
and that he's just seen
something moving in their garden?"
She said, "I mean the one
who's got eyes like blue stars,
hair like golden silk
and a smile like Christmas."

Like I said before —
there's weird fish in this creek.

I began by asking the students what they thought the poem would be about and we focused on the title. Some students thought that it would have something to do with fish. Others thought it might be about something completely different.

Before reading the poem, I asked the students to think, during reading, about what they thought the poet was really trying to say, and why the poet had called the poem "Weird Fish." After reading the poem, I asked what they knew about the boy who was fishing. They said that he didn't like his brother. One student said, "You just get a feeling from the words." When I asked what the brother was like, some of the students said that he's horrible because he's mean — he doesn't like girls and breeds katipo spiders and scares old ladies. Then another student said, "But that doesn't make him horrible because you were only seeing the brother from one point of view — his brother's perspective. From the girl's perspective, the brother was an angel." I asked again why the poet had called the poem "Weird Fish," and one student said that the poet thought the girl was weird because she likes his brother and he knows that he is really a ratbag. Then another student said that the boy in the river really likes the girl and that's why he said all those things about his brother.

These opinions sparked off a lively debate. We had recently been discussing newspaper advertisements and the use of metaphor. This led to the group discussing whether "Weird Fish" was a metaphor. We also looked at the way the poet had used contrast and comparison and had buried ideas in the poem. "The more you read it the clearer it became and the more you got out of it." I then asked the group why they thought the poet had chosen this idea to write about. One student replied, "He's writing about himself. The boy in the river was him. He couldn't come out and say that he really liked the girl, so he wrote about it."

---

56   Vivienne Joseph, "Weird Fish," *School Journal*, Part 4 Number 3 (1981): p. 7

Expository Texts

Expository texts seek to inform, instruct, classify, persuade, and explain. They can stir the imagination as much as any thrilling story, providing facts, theories, or proven explanations about the workings of the social, biological, or physical world. Reading expository texts satisfies a thirst for knowledge and can give enormous pleasure.

You taste your food with your tongue, but the fly does not have a tongue. He tastes his food with his feet and legs. There are little hairs all over his feet and legs. These little hairs help the fly to taste his food.[57]

People live underground in Coober Pedy because it's so hot above ground … Daytime temperatures can reach 50ºC [122ºF]. The ink of ballpoints dries up before you can write on the paper. Metal screws in wooden boxes get so hot that the wood can start to smoke. Drop a live match on the ground and it sometimes bursts into flame.[58]

Some important reasons why students read expository texts in school are to:

- acquire knowledge or information;

- follow instructions;

- seek an explanation;

- follow an argument;

- pursue an interest.

Expository or informational texts are an essential part of a reading program.

Texts as diverse as an article in a magazine, a public notice, a television documentary, a book on earthquakes, a street sign, a library computer database, a report of an accident in the newspaper, or a gossip column in a magazine are all examples of expository writing.

Expository texts present readers with challenges that are often not found in narrative texts. Everyday words are given specialized meanings. Some expository texts are packed with information and contain little repetition to help the reader. Others communicate advice and information clearly, without frills, but in a way that lacks the personal touch; their language is of a generalized public sort.

Teachers, therefore, should not assume that skilled readers of narrative texts can read expository texts as effectively. Tom Nicholson discovered, in his study of high school reading, that many students were having difficulty in reading expository texts — "there was a maze of confusion."[59] The study found that a

---

57 J. W. Leonard, "Flies Taste with their Legs," *Giant Soup,* Ready to Read series (Wellington: Learning Media, 1993)

58 David Hill, "Down Under," *School Journal,* Part 3 Number 3 (1994)

59 Tom Nicholson, "The Confusing World of High School Reading," *Best of SET: Reading* (1985): item 7, p. 1

large gap existed between what the teachers thought their students were understanding and what the students actually understood. Students had difficulty with the specialized vocabulary, the syntax used, and the tables and diagrams in expository texts.

The strategies students learn when reading narrative do not all automatically transfer to other kinds of text. Students may have had less practice in reading expository texts. When they do read them, it is for purposes that are different from those for which they read narrative texts. In addition, the text features of many kinds of expository writing are very different from the familiar text features of narrative writing. This means that reading expository texts often requires the use of additional strategies and understandings, which teachers need to be aware of so that they can consciously model and teach them.

Teachers need to help students to focus on the processes involved in accessing and using information.

Acquiring knowledge about a particular topic is not the sole objective of reading these texts. The teacher needs to focus on the processes involved in accessing and using information. Refer to pages 137–140. Once students have grasped the basic strategies, they can apply them in other learning situations of increasing complexity.

Some Types of Expository Text

	Features	Students should be learning to:
Letters	formal and informal written communication of ideas to another person or organization	distinguish between personal and business letters; understand the conventions of letter writing.
Diaries	records of appointments and things to do recounts of events and/or thoughts and ideas, usually sequential and nearly always private and personal (Sometimes diaries of famous people become available for study.)	discuss the style and type of writing used in diaries; appreciate the voice and tone of the writing, and explain why they are used.
Advertising and propaganda	persuasive announcements in the media or in public places propaganda is usually issued by organized groups in a systematic way	note the different language features used to persuade the reader, for example, vocabulary, register, metaphor; note other features, such as repetition, music, pace, graphics, fonts, color; see the values and concerns behind the text and be able to detect bias; distinguish fact from hype.

	Features	**Students should be learning to:**
Descriptions	give details of things, events, people, and situations may be specific (for example, a report of a particular road accident), or general (for example, a pamphlet on road accidents)	confirm accuracy; distinguish between general and specific descriptions; classify and organize the ideas into hierarchies; summarize the ideas in their own words; understand graphic presentations and symbols, for example, maps and plans.
Explanations	how things work and behave may include details of why things behave as they do	retell the explanation in their own words; summarize the content in their own words; recognize false steps and omissions; understand graphics.
Instructions	a sequence of directions, for example, on how to work a device or cook a meal may be ordered by time (first, next, later) or logic (so that, as a result, in order to)	understand and follow logical sequences, including sequences of instructions often found on labels; understand the conventions in instructions, for example, headings, numbered steps, diagrams, parts named.
Tables	matrices in which information is presented horizontally and vertically (include train and bus timetables, road distance schedules, graphs, score cards, order forms, and so on)	be clear about what information is needed; cross-reference and narrow down the possibilities in the table quickly to comprehend and act on the information.
Forms	documents with blank spaces for information to be inserted (include bank account application forms, dog licenses, competition and library forms, permission slips, and so on)	handle complex sentences, unfamiliar vocabulary, and complex layout.
Arguments	supporting ideas presented in a sequence to justify a particular stand or viewpoint that a writer is taking	summarize the argument in their own words; identify the sequence of ideas; recognize bias and emotive language; distinguish fact from opinion; check the accuracy of the text; understand graphics and symbols used.

	Features	**Students should be learning to:**
Reports	a means of describing and classifying information can be straightforward recounts of events but may be more than this; some may state a problem and suggest a solution; some may argue a case for or against an option and make recommendations	see how the content of the report is divided into parts, for example, • opening statement/problem/need, • cause and effect/consequences, • comparison/contrast, • solution; recognize bias and emotive language; distinguish fact from opinion; check the accuracy of the text; understand graphics, symbols, and other devices used in the text; evaluate the effectiveness of the proposed recommendations or solutions.
Notices and signs	information, instructions, directions, and warnings, usually short and presented in such a way as to attract attention often employ non-verbal features	understand the messages in signs and notices (both informative and persuasive); evaluate the effectiveness of the message, and explain how meaning is created; note abbreviations used, visual or graphic features, and condensed style; make connections between verbal and visual signs.
Catalogs and directories	books or lists of names, items, products, and so on, usually presented alphabetically under headings may be presented in paper form, on microfiche, or be computerized onto databases often use specialized symbols and abbreviations	use alphabetical and numerical ordering with ease; use telephone and street directories, atlases, contents pages, indexes, and databases; become familiar with classification systems, for example, the Dewey system, or using keywords.

Diaries

A diary may be a journal in which personal thoughts or recounts of events are written regularly or occasionally, or it may be a record of appointments and tasks to be completed.

Some diaries are written in an informal style and contain private thoughts not meant to be read by others.

Monday, March 16th

Went to school. Found it closed. In my anguish I had forgotten that I am on holiday. Didn't want to go home, so went to see Bert Baxter instead. He said the social worker had been to see him and had promised to get Sabre a new kennel but he can't have a home help. (Bert, not Sabre.) [60]

At times, personal diaries become public and are read by students when undertaking a research project.

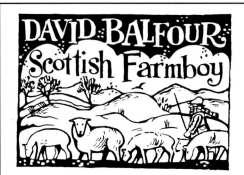

David Balfour was born in Scotland in 1841. He resisted all efforts to make him stay at school, and he started work at an age when most children are in primary school. In his first job he wound up balls of shoemakers' thread. He earned two shillings [20 cents] a week, which was a great help to his parents. His next job was on a property where he turned the handle of a rope-spinning machine. [61]

Tom came down from the mountains with some young sheep to the turnip fields of the lowlands for the winter as the highlands get too much snow for the sheep to be able to live.

Tom took his sheep on from farm to farm through the winter. When they had eaten all the turnips on one he moved them to another and in the spring he took them home again.

David helped Tom with his and decided that looking after was much better than looki cows. When he was thirteen h work on a sheep farm. He w journal many years later:

I watched the sheep in all day and at night inside the sheep nets nets to a new place e

Sheep nets were a fence, and it was the manufacture nets

Other diaries or calendars can be used to record appointments and useful information. These can be consulted by others as well as by the diary owner.

---

60 Sue Townsend, *The Secret Diary of Adrian Mole Aged 13¾* (London: Methuen, 1982), p. 48. This extract reprinted by permission of Reed Consumer Books.

61 K. Mooney, "David Balfour," *School Journal,* Part 4 Number 3 (1978): pp. 32–41

APRIL

Felice coming over

Monday 15

Tuesday 16 ★

Wednesday 17 ★

X Files is on

Thursday 18 ★

Friday 19 ★

Saturday 21 Clarinet lessons

Sunday 20 ★ Grandma for lunch

The Teacher's Role

Students in some schools are asked to keep a diary or journal. Sometimes these are shown to a teacher or shared with friends. The writing can take the form of regular letters exchanged between the student and the teacher. Such writing may be highly personal, expressing individual values without reservation. These diaries provide a basis from which, later, fiction can be written and shared with others.

Reading and studying diaries helps students make distinctions between informal personal accounts of life and feelings, and the useful facts and information that both formal and informal diaries contain. The following activities and questions are suggested.

Thinking Critically

Why do people write diaries?
Select and describe a person you know. Discuss their personality, circumstances, and values, and predict what kind of diary they might keep.
What are the significant things the writer would want to include?
Read and discuss extracts from appropriate diaries.
Why did this person write in this way about these things?
Relate the content of a diary text to background information about the times (for example, relate an immigrant's diary to the history of the time).
What can you find out about the topic from the diary?
Is it possible to authenticate the diary entries?
Encourage the students to consider how vividly diaries can convey the writer's personality and times.

Exploring Language

Discuss with the students any special language features that convey the voice of the writer, or the period when the diary was written.

Building a Language for Discussion

In discussing diaries, teachers will need to note words such as:

- date, planner, schedule, public holiday, moveable feasts …

- notes, name and address, personal details …

- entry, succeeding, previous, following, appointment, visit …

- register, tone, style, personal, impersonal, formal …

- warm, frosty, angry, private, intimate …

Processing Information

Have the students read and create diaries (both personal and formal) as an explorer, scientist, mountaineer, farmer, doctor, or politician.
Look at selected extracts from diaries and pair them with their writers.
Why have you chosen this writer as the probable author of this piece?
After reading or listening to extracts from a diary, describe the author.

Below, one teacher describes how she used diaries in the context of her class program.

A Teacher's Account of Using Diaries

We were preparing to go on camp, and a writing focus for the students was going to be their own diaries. I decided then that reading a variety of diaries would be a good way of introducing the language features of diaries to the students. I already had a copy of *Zlata's Diary*,[62] which the students had heard part of, and some of them had also read *The Diary of Anne Frank.*

I chose some extracts from each diary and photocopied them for the group. Before reading, we discussed and listed the various types of diaries and the different purposes people have for writing them. We also examined what it was that made diaries different from other forms of writing, such as letters, narratives, or reports. We discovered that diaries are generally written in the first person and in the past tense and that they record feelings, events, and experiences. Before we started reading, we shared what we knew about the backgrounds and family circumstances of each of the young authors. I also asked the students to take note of the phrases and words that they thought were features of diary writing.

Through discussion, the students decided that although both the diaries were written by adolescent girls in similar circumstances, their interpretations, and the ways they recorded their own lives and the world around them, were very different. In comparing the styles of these writers, the students discussed things such as different periods, family relationships, and the tensions and stresses of living in a war-torn country. They were really intrigued by the different style and voice of each author. Anne Frank's diary was very full, explicit, and descriptive, while Zlata's diary was factual and direct, with less sophisticated language. They were asked to consider why this was so and whether they could tell if the writing was authentic. This led on to a lively discussion about whether diaries are a true record of events.

For a bit of fun, I shared my own diary written during a recent holiday walking the Heaphy Track. The students were amused by some of my entries. A few days later, some of the students wrote their own responses to my writing in their own writing journals. Their responses were very frank!

---

62 Zlata Filipovik, *Zlata's Diary* (London: Viking, 1994)

Letters

In today's world of rapid communications, there is an increasing need for students to be skilled in reading and writing formal and informal letters. Students need practice and experience in reading and writing different types of letters, faxes, and e-mails, as well as communicating with a wide variety of people.

Personal or private letters will vary enormously in their presentation and style. In formal or business letters, however, a formal register and a special kind of layout are both customary and expected. Students need to become familiar with this register and with the commoner types of layout.

The Teacher's Role

A wide variety of models of letters should be presented to students to help them understand the variety of letters and the conventions and styles of letter-writing. The following activities and questions are suggested.

Kaikorai Primary School

22 Tyne Street,
Roslyn,
Dunedin.

Phone 464-0065
FAX: 03 466 7236

FAX COVER NOTE
TO: Sir/Madam D.C.C
DATE: 17.3.93   NUMBER OF PAGES:

MESSAGE: Dear Sir/Madam,
We feel that the Linden tree should stay.
Here are our reasons why.
We think the tree is too old to cut down.
It is the only linden tree for a long way around.
The area and school used to be called Linden.
Think of the time it took the tree to grow.
There are not many people complaining.
The people have lived there for eight years and only complained half of the time. They knew the tree was there when they bought the house. It gives the area beauty and is a historical landmark.
please don't cut the tree down.

yours faithfully,
Rm. 4
written by Megan, Elspeth and Sam W

Thinking Critically

Ask students to look at particular letters and predict (infer) the nature of the contents from various signals, such as salutation, handwriting or print, signature, and opening or closing sentences.

Why is this person writing? Who is this person writing to?

Does this letter convey its ideas or emotions successfully?

Can you suggest a more effective way that these could be expressed for the reader?

Why are the letters of famous people so valuable?

Exploring Language

Is the language used personal or impersonal? Factual? Persuasive?

Why is the language used in this way? What is the impact on the reader?

Building a Language for Discussion

In discussing letters, teachers will need to help students understand the use of words and terms such as:

first, second, and third person, personal, impersonal, autobiographical, factual, persuasive, e-mail, fax, phone, contact number, address, return address, date, salutation, title, formal, informal, opening, closing, signature, enquiry, application, interview, curriculum vitae, enclosed, cost, payment, repayment, receipt, bill, estimate, quote, response, re, reference, concerning, in reference to, dated, request, reply, inform, require, complain, report, thank you, gratitude, apologize, cancel, confirm.

Processing Information

Have the class respond to a letter and read and share responses. Discuss the way the letter is organized. What are the parts that make up the whole?

Send an e-mail message, or a fax, requesting information on a specific topic. Discuss the reply when it arrives.

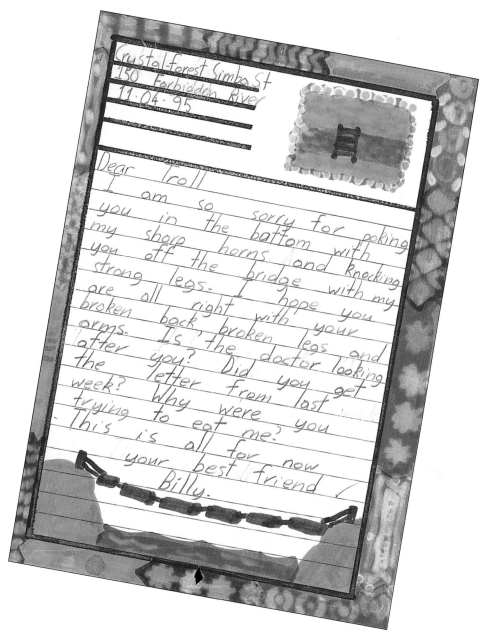

Advertising and Propaganda

"It pays to advertise!" — but the consumer, as well as the manufacturer, can benefit from advertising. We all need information, and sometimes we need to be persuaded, especially when we are asked to try something new. This applies not only to things we might buy in the shops but also to ideas needed to change our local, national, or international policies.

The Teacher's Role

Teachers and students can collect a sample of advertisements and examples of propaganda for students to analyze. Many of the language devices used by writers of advertisements are also used by novelists, poets, and dramatists. The following activities and questions are suggested to help students gain understanding of advertising and the language of propaganda.

Thinking Critically

Display a current poster or an advertisement, an editorial, or a persuasive article, and ask the students to predict its target audience.

What is this poster trying to promote or "sell"? How? To whom? How does it try to grab attention?

Compare the claims of different advertisements for the same kind of product. Have the students discuss their favorite and most hated television commercials, or bring advertisements and propaganda to class, and discuss any that they think are especially attractive, exciting, persuasive, or awful. Encourage them to give reasons for their judgments.

Does this advertisement use any emotionally loaded words or phrases?

Can you tell whether what is said is fact or opinion? If so, how?

Students can learn to detect bias by listing or highlighting persuasive words and phrases used in advertisements and viewpoint articles (such as editorials) and can begin to distinguish facts from opinions.

Is the voice used colloquial in tone? Or formal? Or literary?
Ask students to analyze register (tone) in common posters, graffiti, or television commercials, to show the writer's attitude towards the reader.

Exploring Language

Students can sort advertisements into categories. For example, they can categorize them according to content, effectiveness, look, tone, pace or urgency, style, and use of images, including metaphors. Each category should be named. *What metaphors or other images are used? How effective are they?*
List and classify text features of advertisements by their meanings, their shapes, their spellings, their sentence length, their unusual phrases, their structures and abbreviated language structures, their typography and layout, their visual images, and their use of sounds and rhythms.
Analyze the logical development of a viewpoint article, such as an editorial.

Building a Language for Discussion

Today's customers, voters, media watchers, and readers of the daily paper need to have one eye open for the facts, and the other on how the facts are presented. Our advertising ploys and propaganda demonstrate our values and concerns. Students need to learn to recognize the persuasive use of language and format, to note words commonly used in advertising, and to discuss the differences between advertising and propaganda.

Advertising includes:

- words for urgent action — now, at once;

- positive concepts — *new, fresh, whole, good, cheap, real, warm, free, lovely, perfect, luxurious, practical …*

- personal address — **YOU** *need this;*

- comparative or superlative forms of adjectives and adverbs;

- colorful comparisons;

- simple structures that are familiar, such as imperatives — *Buy it now!*

- abbreviated structures — *Experience the sensation of walking on air! Cools the feet, helps prevent odor;*

- hyperbole — *The world's most wanted car!*

- metaphor and imagery — *Light thin crackers, thin as air!*

- constant repetition of the brand name or idea;

- colloquialisms or slang;

- strings of modifiers (often hyphenated) before the nouns — *Cool, tingly, thirst-quenching lemonade; Space-saving, slot-together kitsets;*

- nouns formed from abbreviated sentence structures — *Forget outsourcing.*
  Forget rehiring. Give your own staff the skills needed to go client-server.

In propaganda, the writer's goal is usually to change attitudes rather than to evaluate a large number of complex facts. Propaganda appeals to people's underlying bias or bigotry rather than to their informed judgment. Readers often come across persuasive language in "viewpoint" columns or in newspaper editorials. Although the writer can make use of some of the tricks of advertising, these kinds of text are fairly formal, and most do not employ abbreviations or slang. The vocabulary is generally appropriate to the topic. Some facts are included to support the opinions put forward. Persuasion is often much more subtle than in the language of advertising and can create an attitude of belief in the reader.

Compared with advertising, propaganda relies more on the organization of ideas and on rhetorical devices, such as frequent repetition or patterned language structures to build up to a climax. Propaganda can use language and visual images to express positive ideas in an inspiring way.

I have a dream that one day on the red hills of Georgia, the sons of former slaves and the sons of former slave-owners will be able to sit down together at a table of brotherhood. I have a dream that one day, even the state of Missouri, a desert state, sweltering with the heat of injustice and oppression, will be transformed into an oasis of freedom and justice. I have a dream that my four children will one day live in a nation where they will not be judged by the color of their skin but by the content of their character.

I have a dream today! ...[63]

Processing Information

Make up advertisements and editorials on a product or topic, and compare and discuss results. Innovate on known examples.

Reword information as an advertisement or an editorial viewpoint.

Discuss the elements of a number of advertisements. Explore how visual and verbal elements are conveyed and combined.

---

63 Extract from speech given by Martin Luther King on August 28, 1963, by the Lincoln Memorial, Washington. Source: World Wide Web "I have a dream" by Martin Luther King Jr. [online]. Available from ftp://ftp.msstate.edu/pub/docs/history/USA/Afro-Amer/dream.king

Descriptions

Descriptions are verbal pictures of people, situations, objects, or other things. They usually have an order or framework and are either specific or general. For example, a student might read an account of a road accident in the newspaper. This is a specific kind of description. Another kind of description could feature the same topic in a general way, for example, in a pamphlet on road accidents.

The Teacher's Role

Students will read many descriptions for interest and information. Each one they read will serve as a model, showing them ways of organizing and arranging descriptive ideas that they can then use in their own writing.

It is useful for readers to compare the descriptions they meet in literary texts with those in expository texts. One way in which they can distinguish between an objective description and a subjective one is by looking for emotive words, which signal a subjective approach.

Students can be helped to read descriptions and explanations more closely through the following questions and activities.

Thinking Critically

Talk about the topic, asking:

- *What do I already know about … ?*

- *What do I want to find out?*

- *What is the purpose of writing a description?*

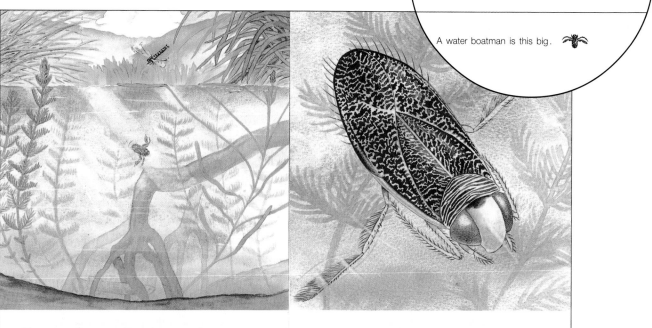

The Water Boatman

compound eye   wings   fine hairs   front leg   middle leg   back leg

A water boatman is this big.

The water boatman lives in a pond.

It swims with its back legs.

127

Do you think the information is accurate? How can you check it?

Decide whether a selected description is meant to inform you or make you feel an emotion (that is, whether it is objective or subjective). Give reasons for your decision.

Is a description the best way of presenting this information?

Draw a picture or diagram of something while listening to a description of it.

Explain how the information in an account or description is ordered.

Exploring Language

Consider a particular description.

What are the language features that tell you this is a description?

Decide whether the information refers to one object or a group of similar objects.

What is this description or explanation about?

Find a part that describes the shape, color, texture, size, function, or location of something.

How does the layout help readers to find the information easily?

Building a Language for Discussion

Teachers will need to introduce specialized vocabulary related to the subject of the description and encourage students to note:

* shape, size, color, and texture words;

* function words and verbs of action (*spins, fits, lives, hunts, eats*);

* location words, including prepositions and prepositional phrases (*underground, above, in the canopy, at sea, on the shoreline*);

* duration and frequency words, including time adverbs and prepositional phrases of time (*every year, usually, frequently, never, by night, in the winter*);

* words indicating sequence, including time-related conjunctions, time and place prepositions (*after, until, as soon as, when*);

How we can tell that it's a bumble bee?

1 - it's got black and yellow stripes.
2 - it's fat.
3 - It makes a buzzing noise.
4 - they go on flowers
5 - it's got wings like a cicada.
6 - it's got a pointy tail.
7 - it looks fluffy.
8 - It flies around flowers.
9 - a bumble bee is bigger than a wasp.
10 - it's got six legs.

Na Tiffany Walker

- words indicating manner, including adverbs and prepositional phrases of manner *(quickly, on its stomach, with its head erect)*;

- words indicating relationship, including prepositions and prepositional phrases, verbs, and nouns *(system, organization, group, relates to, is part of, works under, is affected by, reports to)*;

- words and phrases relating to layout *(tree diagram, branch, box, column, row, caption, heading, subheading)*.

Processing Information

Ask students to present information in another form, for example, by turning a brainstorm or semantic web into a tree diagram or structured overview. (This activity is easier when a clear focus has been provided for the original brainstorm.)

Ask students to choose a common object and make a description of it, for a chosen audience and in a chosen form. For example, the audience could be a child, a scientist, or a general-interest reader; the form could be a hierarchy, a prose description, a table, a directory, a diagram, or a map.

Instructions

Recipes, instructions, and timetables are so commonplace that we tend to take them for granted. They tell us how to behave, how to operate and make things, and what to do in emergencies. Many of these texts need to be read carefully because the reader has to be clear about exactly what they mean. It could be a matter of life or death.

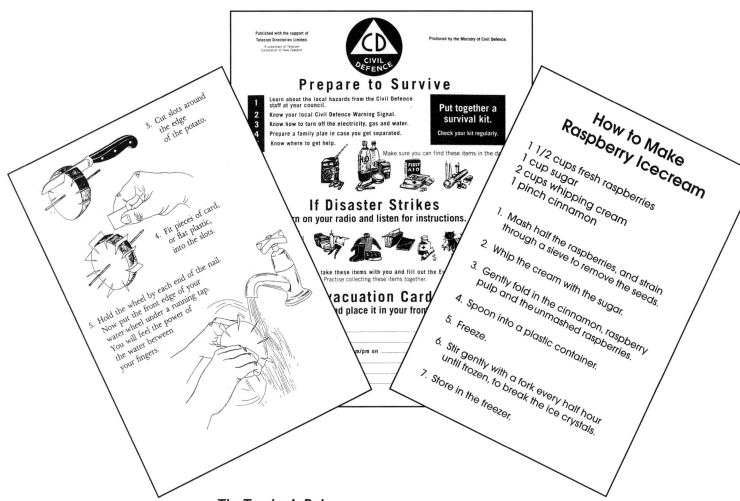

The Teacher's Role

Ask the students to explain what instructions are, where we can expect to find them, and how they are used in everyday life. Have them bring examples from home to share. One of the best ways of learning to evaluate sets of instructions is to try creating a set, then getting someone else to carry them out. This experience can demonstrate the strengths and weaknesses of particular ways of expressing instructions.

Students can be helped to understand and follow instructions more easily through the following questions and activities.

Thinking Critically

Read a set of instructions (which may be a form or table that needs filling in), note places where you find difficulties, and suggest solutions.

What is the purpose of this set of instructions?
What makes the instructions difficult to understand?
How do these parts work? or *What do you put here?*
Are there diagrams or captions? Do they help you understand?
Read labels on medicine bottles or household products.
Are there any warnings?

> **NOT TO BE TAKEN**
> **GLYCERINE THYMOL CO**
> Use one teaspoon in half a glass of warm water as a mouthwash three times daily.

Exploring Language

Share examples of a variety of instructions that students use or that are needed in daily life. Ask the students:

- *Is the sequence of action or method clearly set out?*

- *Does the layout of the text help make the instructions easy to understand? (Are steps numbered or listed?)*

- *Are the materials listed in order of use?*

- *What words are used for linking the text (first, when, then)?*

Building a Language for Discussion

Instructions include size, shape, color, and texture descriptions appropriate to the thing being made or the procedure being followed. Draw students' attention to the imperative use of verbs to command the reader (for example, "Run twice round the block" or "Put in a cup of sugar.") In addition, teachers and students will need to note words and phrases such as:

- heading, title, subtitle, purpose, goal, sequence, step, stage, follow, go to, go back, see diagram, recipe, manual, operating instructions …

- first, next, when, after, as soon as, etc., in, on, at, under, through, at the side of …

- factual, ordered, logical …

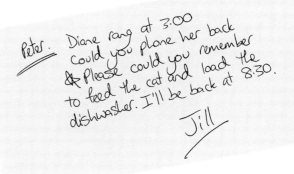

Processing Information

Design instructions for playing a board game, using graphics where appropriate.
Give verbal instructions about familiar processes, for example, making a bed, riding a bike, making a cup of hot chocolate. Have someone carry out some of these instructions if appropriate. Make a flow chart or diagram of the sequence. Play Chinese Whispers with a set of instructions. The last person to listen to the message carries out the instructions as received.

Arguments

The skill of following an argument (and rebutting it when necessary) is one that all students need to learn. Students can present their own ideas more clearly in writing if they can follow someone else's line of thought in their reading. Those who can make effective written submissions for or against a case often gain more power in our society.

The Teacher's Role

Teachers need to help readers become confident in understanding arguments and responding to them. Provide students with good models, presenting arguments for and against, such as in the example below.[64] Students can be helped to read arguments through the following activities and questions.

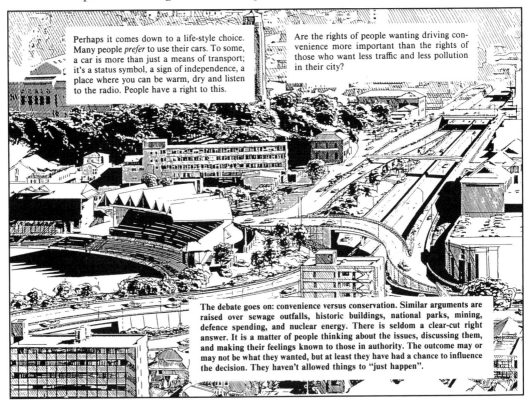

Perhaps it comes down to a life-style choice. Many people *prefer* to use their cars. To some, a car is more than just a means of transport; it's a status symbol, a sign of independence, a place where you can be warm, dry and listen to the radio. People have a right to this.

Are the rights of people wanting driving convenience more important than the rights of those who want less traffic and less pollution in their city?

The debate goes on: convenience versus conservation. Similar arguments are raised over sewage outfalls, historic buildings, national parks, mining, defence spending, and nuclear energy. There is seldom a clear-cut right answer. It is a matter of people thinking about the issues, discussing them, and making their feelings known to those in authority. The outcome may or may not be what they wanted, but at least they have had a chance to influence the decision. They haven't allowed things to "just happen".

Thinking Critically

How is an argument in writing different from an argument in conversation? Why would someone want to write an argument?

Trace an argument by identifying the main ideas and the supporting ideas in each paragraph.

What is the first sentence about? Is this the main idea of the paragraph?

---

64 From "The Motorway Debate," by Pat Quinn, illustration by Transit New Zealand (*School Journal*, Part 4 Number 1, 1992), p. 31

Do you think the proposed solution will work? Do you think the writer's conclusion is valid? Justify your opinion.

Read the first sentence or sentences of a "viewpoint" article, and predict what the rest of the text will be about.

Select a controversial topic, such as whether people should be allowed to own guns. Propose two very different solutions and ask people to take one side or the other. Compare and discuss the arguments for each side and decide whether one solution is better, or whether there might be another even better way of solving the problem.

Choose a newspaper article that expresses concern about a family-related topic. *What theory, argument, or problem is put forward? Why is the writer concerned? Are there any places where you find the argument hard to follow?*

Exploring Language

How is the text arranged (sequence, supporting ideas, summary)?
Does the writer use emotive words? Repetition?
What tense is the argument written in — past, present, or future?

Pick out examples showing how the main idea is elaborated or intensified, and highlight key words.

Highlight words that add information.

Identify the connecting (link) words or expressions.

Building a Language for Discussion

Teachers can discuss with students words that are especially relevant to particular arguments, as well as words such as:

- evidence, fact, objective, subjective, theory, opinion, proof, example, alternative, true, false, prejudice, bias;

- viewpoint, elaboration, restriction;

- cause and effect, problem and solution;

- compare and contrast.

"Viewpoint" words include:

- personally; in my opinion; people say; they told me that; it seems that; I think that; it is said that; from our point of view; the theory is that; the fact is; technically speaking; officially, of course; in fact; really; certainly; indeed.

Often the choice of noun or adjective shows the viewpoint of the writer. For example, to talk of minke whales as "sea rats" clearly indicates an attitude. Language markers for comparison and contrast include:

- but; instead; on the contrary; by comparison; -er; -est; more; most; on the other hand; in the same way; likewise; similarly; other; different; varied; unlike.

Processing Information

Make a summary of the argument you have read. (This could be done in groups.)

Find any evidence for the argument and check it for accuracy.

Determine whether an argument is logical by reordering the paragraphs from a cut-up text.

Check ideas and facts by comparing them with fixed standards (for example, the exact depth of snow in a certain place on a certain day, or the actual date when something occurred).

Role-play the argument or turn it into a debate, using points made in the text.

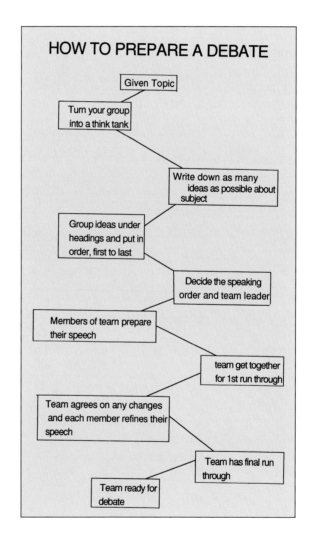

Reports

Reports can be straightforward recounts of events, but many of them are more than this. They may contain accounts and descriptions, but they often do more than describe a thing, event, or situation. Some reports state a problem and suggest a solution. Some argue a case for or against a particular option, supporting their case with evidence and making a recommendation.

The Teacher's Role

Teachers need to help readers become confident in understanding and dealing with reports. Students can be helped to read this type of expository writing through the following suggested questions and activities.

Thinking Critically

What would be some topics we could write a report about?
What is special about reports? Can you identify reports in any of your own writing?
Consider a report by another writer.
What is the report about? Does it state a position or problem or discuss an event?
Does the way the author has grouped together ideas or information help you find out more about the topic?

Exploring Language

What are the language features that tell you something is a report?
If you wanted to present some information about a topic in written form so that others could learn from it, how would you put your ideas together?
Examine a particular report.
How has the author presented the ideas? Is the information in the report easy to locate and interpret? If so, how has the author achieved this? Can you distinguish facts from opinion, in the report? If so, which words help you?

Building a Language for Discussion

Teachers can discuss with students words especially relevant to the topics of particular reports and also words used to discuss reports, such as:

- evidence, fact, objective, neutral, subjective, theory, opinion, proof, example, alternative, true, false, prejudice, bias;

- viewpoint, elaboration, restriction;

Field assistant Stuart Hildreth (left) and survey technician Phillip Stroud check the rails protruding from the Museum Hotel preparing for the big shift. Picture: JOHN NICHOLSON

3000-tonne shift

HOTEL ON THE MOVE

The Museum Hotel is to shift this weekend. **Annette Finnegan** looks at what possessed a man to move a 3000-tonne building.

IT began over lunch. A Wellington steak bar spawned the idea for the biggest building move in New Zealand history.

Museum Hotel mover Chris Parkin and neighbour Cameron Shaw in June 1992 sat eating their weekly steak and chips.

"I was discussing the fact the

Government had given the Museum of New Zealand the final go ahead and commiserating that would probably be the end of the hotel operation," Mr Parkin said.

Said Mr Shaw: "Why don't you move it?"

Mr Parkin was involved in a joint venture which had been running the hotel in 1990. He decided to research the idea.

Nothing much happened until late 1992 when the Museum of New Zealand project office gave Mr Parkin's group notice to quit the hotel to make way for the new museum.

CONTINUES page 3

SEE PAGE 3

Reproduced courtesy of *The Evening Post.*

- cause and effect, problem and solution;

- compare and contrast.

Language "markers" that indicate comparison or contrast include:

- but; instead; on the contrary; by comparison; -er/-est; more/most; on the other hand; in the same way; likewise; similarly; other; different; varied; unlike.

Processing Information

What are other ways in which the author could have presented this information?
Do you think you have found out a lot about this topic by reading this report?
Tell someone how to write a newspaper report, weather report, or science report.

Here is a description of how one teacher explored the language and structure of weather reports.

A Teacher's Account of Looking at Weather Reports

In science we were investigating patterns of weather and using data to predict the weather. I decided that the students needed to read and understand the signs and symbols, as well as the language, of weather reports and maps.

With this in mind, I asked the students to collect a variety of weather maps from the newspapers for a week so that we could come to grips with their special features.

We first needed to identify what we thought was the purpose of writing weather forecasts and who the audience was. We discussed what sort of writing was needed to give people information on any given topic, and the students said things like:

"The writing needs to be clear so that no one gets confused."

"It is factual writing."

"You have to use special words."

"You have to write about what's true."

I asked the students what they thought would be the difference between other reports and a weather report. One student said: "Weather reports are different because they tell us what has happened and they also tell us what will probably happen, but they're often wrong!"

We then talked about how scientists predict weather and why the weather reports are sometimes wrong. The students went on to plan and create their own methods for measuring wind direction and wind speed and for identifying and interpreting clouds.

Back to the reading!

We read a variety of written weather reports in the newspaper and discussed the way they were written. We looked carefully at the sentence structures and the sorts of words and phrases that were used to convey information. The students discovered that several words and phrases were common to all weather reports. We listed these words and, in pairs, the students wrote their own understandings of the features of weather reports.

They also wrote their own interpretation of such words and phrases as "flow of moist air," "a high-pressure system," "extending," "cold front," "warm front," "high" and "low," "accumulation of snow," and "mostly sunny."

This gave us a base to work from. We then spent some time trying out our definitions in the context of real weather reports. The students also wrote their own weather reports. We shared them together and displayed them for others to read.

Processing Information

To make efficient and effective use of information in expository texts, readers must be able to use the strategies of deciding, locating, using, recording, presenting, and reflecting.

Deciding on a Purpose

The teacher's first and most important task is to make sure that readers know why they are looking for information on a particular topic. This purpose should be clearly established at the beginning. For example, a student may have questions about a topic — finding answers to these questions is their purpose for reading.

Through skillful questioning, the teacher will be able to draw from the students what they already know about the topic. Discussion questions might include:

- *What do you already know?*

- *What do you need to know?*

- *Where can you find it?*

Locating Appropriate Resources

When prior knowledge has been established, the student will have a familiar base on which to build further questions. Brainstorm to identify key words and related words, so that wider sources of information (for example, atlases or dictionaries) can be used. Make a note of questions and the kinds of resources students need and where they should go to find them. This will give the student a framework within which to work. A simple pathfinder or advance organizer, like the one shown on this page, can be used to clarify the steps to follow.

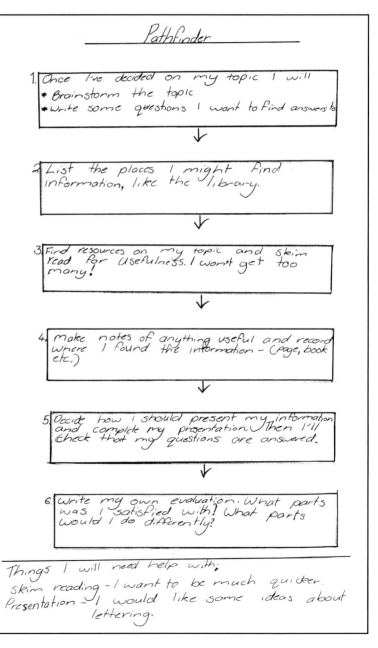

Students need to be aware of the wide variety of resources available to them and know where to find them. It is helpful to ask:

- *Will I find the information in magazines, newspaper articles, or on the World Wide Web, or is it well documented in books?*

- *Do I have to ask a business or local community organization to send this information?*

- *Can I get this information from the class or school library? Is it on CD-ROM?*

Students also need to check the accuracy of the information they locate. Questions they might ask include:

- *Who is the writer?*

- *Does the writer know the subject well?*

- *Is this text the best one to provide answers to my questions?*

- *Is the text up to date?*

- *Is the writer stating facts or personal opinions?*

- *How do I know that the writer is telling the truth?*

- *Can the information be validated? (That is, can I find the same information in other resources?)*

Using the Resources

Inexperienced readers often gather a large number of resources — more than they need or can effectively manage. Teachers can discuss and demonstrate how resources may be culled to an appropriate number.

The questions a reader asks initially may be rather general, because the reader as yet knows little about the topic. For example, a student studying cats might ask:

- *What food do cats eat?*

As students acquire new information, they redefine and clarify their questions, thus reducing the amount of information required to a manageable level. For example:

- *What kind of food do kittens eat?*

When specific questions have been established, the teacher can focus on key words and related words, listing these to help readers locate information about the topic. Teachers can show how to use an index (if there is one) to check whether the key words appear somewhere in resource books. Readers can then check whether the word is mentioned just in passing, or whether the reference takes up several pages, and they can note the length of each reference (for example, "kittens, pages 20 to 27; feeding, page 22.")

The table of contents and chapter headings in a book, or the directory of a computer or newspaper, can also be used to show readers how to predict whether the information is contained in specific parts or sections. By simply using an index and table of contents, readers can see that some resources contain more pertinent information than others.

Other factors that will help students decide whether the resource is appropriate include:

- level (*Can I read this material? If not, who can help me to read it?*)

- content (*Is it on my topic?*)

- specialized vocabulary (*Are there too many unfamiliar words for me to cope with? If so, what can I do about it?*)

- context clues (*Are new words and ideas explained in the text? If not, what other things, such as a glossary, can help me?*)

- organization of the text (*Is the information laid out clearly so that I can quickly locate what I need?*).

Readers can scan the text briefly to find out whether it seems "user friendly," that is, whether it provides the required information in a way that is easy to use.

Recording the Information

Once they have decided which information is appropriate to their requirements, readers can extract it in one form or another, for example, in a timeline, a table, a web, jottings, or lists.

HYPOTHERMIA

POSSIBLE SIGNS	POSSIBLE CAUSES	TREATMENT	PREVENTION	POINTS 2 REMEMBER
Cold / Shivering

Person may feel exhausted and clumsy.

Slurred speech difficulty in seeing things.

Irrational behaviour

Lack of interest

Some signs of progressed hypothermia are coma collapse and unconsciousness | The cold, temperature drops with the altitude.

The wind blows away the heat

Wet clothing - because it prevents good insulation

Some contributing factors are

the lack of food

fatigue lack of fitness, too heavy a load.

Recent illness | Prevent further heat loss.

Assist them with warming up.

Find shelter/get out of wind.

Get victim into dry clothes.

Do not give the victim alcohol.

Keep in horizontal recovery position

Warm hot drinks are only a help when victim is conscious. | Wear good warm clothing - preferably wool.

Eat high energy foods.

Have the excursion planned with time for breaks.

Have liquids with you - hot ones.

Don't carry loads that are too heavy for you

Watch for changes in the weather. | Hypothermia can kill anybody; the young and old even the fit and healthy

It's best to have four or more people in your tramping party so one can stay with the victim while two go for help.

If one person has symptoms, others in the party may also have hypothermia. |

Kylie   Information from NZ Mountain Safety Council Pamphlet

Readers may have several references noted down. They can decide which ones will meet their needs by:

- rereading fragments to refresh their memories;

- reflecting on the information gathered;

- redefining the questions they asked initially, since the growth of their knowledge may make the original questions too broad.

Readers will probably need help in deciding on the best way of collating their information and arranging the material in the form of notes, plans for writing, or some other form. To develop the skill of summarizing, it is sometimes helpful to have the readers recount the basic information in their own words. All the above extraction techniques need to be taught, particularly the skill of note-taking.

Once readers have decided what is relevant information, they are ready to use it.

Presenting the Information

Before presenting information, readers must pass it through their own minds and evaluate it, so that they produce it in a form that they have understood themselves. Teachers will need to determine the depth of understanding gained. Have students truly grasped the message behind the words? Do they understand the main and supporting ideas? Or are they merely regurgitating words they saw on the page?

From a very young age, readers can be encouraged to put what they have read, or had read to them, into their own words. In the example shown here, a story about an endangered bird, the kakapo, has been retold by an eight-year-old.

Readers can assess the value of the information they find in any one resource and compare it with their own experience, with what they have already learned, and with what they find out from several other sources. They can also check that their information does not contain a hidden bias.

Students have a range of options for presentation through which they can demonstrate the knowledge, skills, and attitudes they have gained. They can

There were not many kakapo left, so some scientists thought they would help by giving them extra food to make them strong. If the birds were strong they could have babies.

present their information in written, oral, and visual form, using appropriate technologies. In assessing, teachers and students should take account of the presentation methods students have used.

Reflecting on What Has Been Learned

Throughout the whole process of reading and retrieving information from expository texts, students can reflect on various aspects of their experience. Finally, they will evaluate what they have learned. Questions they may ask themselves include:

- *What new information do I know about the topic?*

- *Can I put it into my own words?*

- *What new retrieval skills have I learned?*

- *Can I use some of my new skills by myself next time?*

- *Were my questions answered?*

- *How has my thinking changed?*

- *How can I use my new learning in future?*

- *Did I present my ideas effectively to others?*

- *How did my audience respond?*

- *What did I find difficult?*

- *Would I do it the same way next time?*

- *Do I want to pursue this topic further?*

- *Did I enjoy this? What did I like best?*

The next time students are seeking information, they can incorporate the new skills and learning that they have gained from working through the processes described above.

7 Organizing for Reading

Organizing for Reading

Organizing for reading should have one overriding purpose — to enable the teacher to provide purposeful, worthwhile reading experiences for all the students in the class. Good class management allows the teacher to monitor students, to model, and to withdraw groups for instruction, conferences, and shared or guided reading without being interrupted. Good class management allows the students plenty of time to read and write, time to talk about books, and access to a wide variety of texts.

The Social Environment

The atmosphere of the classroom affects the quality and rate of students' learning. A warm, supportive classroom environment — one in which each learner's contributions are respected and in which co-operation between students is encouraged — enhances learning. In such an environment, students will be selecting and reading for enjoyment and information.

A classroom should be a community of readers, where people talk over what they have read, recommend books, CD-ROMs, magazines, or newspaper articles to one another, and discuss them, sometimes disagreeing with one another's judgments and sometimes sharing a common response. Discussing people's different responses to text can enhance the experience and understanding of the whole group. Having a time to share is an important aspect of a stimulating and challenging reading program. Young readers enjoy talking over the content of texts and making judgments about their value. As they do so, the students develop their understanding and their critical thinking skills.

The Physical Environment

Schools and classrooms that are full of books and students' writing, as well as displays, charts, and other visual texts, are places in which all kinds of reading can flourish. A rich learning environment will mirror the students' interests and needs and affirm their backgrounds and cultures. It will also contain:

- a variety of texts that represent an appropriate balance of genres;

- an attractive and accessible class library, including, for example, library books, poetry cards, students' published work, maps, pamphlets, and leaflets;

- students' own work in various forms;

- charts, a news board, wall stories, notices, or reports, labeled clearly and placed where students can see them;

- information and communication technologies such as a computer, a fax machine, a cassette recorder, an overhead projector, a listening post, and a video recorder and monitor.

Initial Setting Up

The Beginning of the School Year

At the beginning of the school year, students should be welcomed into a well-organized and well-set-up classroom. When the students arrive, many teachers appeal to them for help, advice, and co-operation in making the classroom more their own. In an environment like this, the students will know they are valued. Right from the start, they will appreciate the significance of language and see school as an interesting and exciting place. As the year progresses, students' own writing and displays will replace much of the material initially provided by the teacher.

When setting up the room, teachers should be sure to make available a wide variety of texts. These could include:

- stories, poetry, plays;

- descriptions, articles, summaries, reports;

- instructions, rules, signs;

- chants, rhymes, songs, jingles;

- personal letters or notes to others;

- biographies, family trees;

- items from newspapers, magazines, pamphlets, and brochures.

Establishing Routines

Start immediately with whole-class activities, such as reading to the class, shared reading, and sustained silent reading. The teacher needs to make lots of different materials available that will appeal to the students. These will include enlarged texts, library books, books from home, audiotapes, poetry cards, and songs.

All kinds of reading and writing activities — shared reading, buddy reading, writing stories and poems, and using the class library — need to be modeled early in the program so that the students can work independently.

Teachers can model:

- appropriate behavior when working in small groups;

- working with a buddy;

- what to do when you have finished;

- reading in the class library;

- independent reading and writing;

- how to move around the classroom;

- an appropriate noise level;

- finding, using, and replacing materials;

- what to do when you need help.

Once classroom routines and procedures are firmly established, the teacher needs to ensure that there are a variety of activities that students can do on their own. These activities must be as purposeful and valuable for the students as those they do when they are withdrawn for individual or group instruction. Learning should be occurring all the time, not just when students are interacting with the teacher.

Independent learning experiences include finding information, looking up a computer database, sharing a book, using the listening post or class library, taking notes, presenting ideas to a group, and holding interviews. (For further suggestions, see pages 87–9.)

When all class members are working without distracting others, the teacher can begin to withdraw groups or individual students for conferences or instruction to:

- talk about a favorite book;

- establish a student's knowledge about book and print conventions;

- discuss a particular text with a group of students;

- take a running record;

- observe students reading independently;

- listen to individual students read, and discuss their reading habits, attitudes, and interests with them;

- take guided reading.

During this time, the teacher can begin to build comprehensive pictures of the reading patterns of individual students and also of the reading levels of the class as a whole. This information can be used to plan for further teaching.

As the year progresses, the students gain confidence in using the routines and structures of the classroom.

Grouping

Groups are created for many different reasons and range in size from one student and the teacher to the whole class. Students may be grouped with others of similar interests or abilities.

The composition of groups needs to be carefully considered and monitored, so that students are placed where they are challenged but not frustrated. Changing groupings makes it less likely that students will be "labeled" as members of a particular group. Low-achieving readers often have valuable contributions to make in self-chosen groups during shared reading and shared writing or when they draw on any special knowledge or background experience.

In a classroom where grouping is flexible, students can form groups of their own spontaneously to pursue activities such as investigating a topic, writing a report, or reading a play. Working in groups:

- allows greater participation by individuals;

- encourages co-operative learning;

- makes effective use of limited resources;

- makes management easier;

- allows in-depth teacher-directed instruction;

- provides opportunities for monitoring students;

- extends or challenges students at a particular level.

Contracts

Students may have their own plan to follow for the day as they work within groups and independently. Sometimes students can formally contract to undertake specific learning activities.

Contracts are formal arrangements between the teacher and an individual, group, or class, where the student or students undertake to reach specified objectives. Contracts have found favor with many teachers and students in recent years.

The teacher or the student writes a contract based on learning objectives that are appropriate for the student's current learning needs. Students state what they intend to learn and the time frame in which the learning will be completed. Once both parties have agreed on the goal and the wording, the contract is signed. Teacher and students monitor progress while the contract is carried out. As the students complete their work, it should be shared and evaluated.

The contract form:

CONTRACT	
Name	Miriam
Date	4·3·97
@Writing@	
Write a book review on Freaky Facts	✓
Buddy read with my friend Juan	✓
Silent Reading	
Title Spain Pages 4-29	✓
Read with the teacher on the mat.	✓
Do 2 skills cards Spelling card 5, printing card 11.	✓ ←
Teacher's signature E.R. St. John.	
Child's signature Miriam	

The Teacher's Role in a Well-managed Classroom

The teacher should be able to move around among individuals and groups, reading along with some, sharing the high point of an exciting story, acknowledging some students' attempts to solve reading problems, asking questions to lead some closer to the meaning, or helping a student find something of interest to read. After this, the teacher can go on to work in a concentrated way with a group of students, taking guided reading or a running record. Throughout this time, the whole class is involved in valuable learning experiences. Such a program gives the teacher the chance to work with all the students as individuals, while the students are learning to read as adults read — for a real and satisfying purpose.

The School Library

The library should be the center for information resources and media in the school. All students should have ready access to their school library, and their experiences there should be positive. Support should be provided so that they quickly become confident, informed, and independent library users. The school library needs to be set up and arranged in the most user-friendly way possible.

Organization of the Library

The school library should be organized in line with standard library procedures so that students who have learned to use this library will be able to use other libraries with confidence.

- All fiction should be organized in alphabetical order by author's surname and shelved from top to bottom and from left to right.

- All non-fiction should be organized according to the Dewey decimal classification system and shelved from top to bottom and from left to right.

- Each school library should have a database of the library collection, preferably on a computer and easy for all students to access.

- Information technology, including CD-ROM texts, videos, cassette recorders, computer databases, and listening posts, should be readily accessible to students in the library.

- Picture books should be kept in upright shelves so that they can be placed with their covers facing outwards.

- Color coding should be used to distinguish picture books from chapter books and novels and also to distinguish between the various Dewey categories.

The library collection should consist only of materials that are attractive, up to date, and likely to be well used. The collection should include resources that reflect the interests and backgrounds of the students. Both teachers and students need to have an input into selecting resources to be purchased for the library. The reading tastes of the students will vary considerably, and teachers need to acknowledge this and be careful not to rely on preconceived judgments about students' reading interests.

The Library Environment

The library ought to be one of the most attractive places in the school. It should include places where students can relax and read on cushions, beanbags, or comfortable chairs. There should also be some good work areas in a quiet part of the library, with chairs and tables or desks where students can study and refer to non-fiction material. Visual displays, perhaps of material by different classes, can make a huge difference to the interest students take in the library. Above all, the library should be a place where all students feel comfortable and can use the resources easily.

A successful school library is one that is an integral part of the school's teaching and learning program. Library services should be available for as much of the day as possible to as many students as possible. Schools that value independent learning make it a priority to give students access to the library in their leisure time.

Communicating with Parents and Caregivers

Organizing for reading should include involvement of parents and caregivers. Students, teachers, and parents all make valuable contributions to students' learning, and a close working relationship between the teacher and the students' parents or caregivers is essential. The better the communication, the more the student will benefit. There are a number of ways for home and school to keep in touch. These include:

Parents are a valuable resource to support students' reading development.

- an "open door" policy;

- arranged interviews;

- individual notes and letters;

- opportunities for parents and caregivers to assist in the classroom, the library, and the school;

- teachers making specific times available for discussion;

- a classroom newsletter;

- meet-the-teacher evenings;

- meetings that focus on the reading curriculum;

- meetings for consultation with the school community when the school's reading program statements are being revised.

It is important for the school to arrange meetings with parents and caregivers to discuss how reading is taught and how parents can assist their children with reading.

149

References

Adams, M. J. *Beginning to Read: Thinking and learning about print.* Cambridge, Massachusetts: MIT Press, 1990.

Ashton-Warner, S. *Teacher.* London: Secker and Warburg, 1963.

Assessment: Policy to practice. Wellington: Learning Media, 1994.

Atwell, N. *In the Middle — Writing, Reading, and Learning with Adolescents.* Portsmouth, New Hampshire: Heinemann, 1987.

Bolton, F. and Snowball, D. *Teaching Spelling.* Portsmouth, New Hampshire: Heinemann, 1993.

Butler, D. *Babies Need Books.* 3rd ed. London: Penguin, 1995, and Portsmouth, New Hampshire: Heinemann, 1997.

Cairney, T. H. *Other Worlds: The endless possibilities of literature.* South Melbourne: Nelson, 1990.

Cambourne, B. *The Whole Story: Natural learning and the acquisition of literacy in the classroom.* Auckland: Ashton Scholastic, 1988.

Cazden, C. *Classroom Discourse: The language of teaching and learning.* Portsmouth, New Hampshire: Heinemann, 1988.

Clay, M. M. *An Observation Survey of Early Literacy Achievement.* Auckland: Heinemann, 1993.

Clay, M. M. *Becoming Literate: The construction of inner control.* Auckland: Heinemann, 1991.

Clay, M. M. *What Did I Write?* Auckland: Heinemann Educational, 1975.

Dancing with the Pen: The learner as a writer. Wellington: Learning Media, 1993.

Derewianka, B. *Exploring How Texts Work.* Rozelle, NSW: Primary English Teaching Association, 1990.

Donaldson, M. *Children's Minds.* London: Croom Helm, 1978.

Elley, W. B. *How in the World Do Students Read?* New York: International Association for the Evaluation of Educational Achievement, 1992.

English in the New Zealand Curriculum. Wellington: Learning Media, 1994.

Exploring Language: A handbook for teachers. Wellington: Learning Media, 1996.

Fountas, I. and Pinnell, G. S. *Guided Reading.* Portsmouth, New Hampshire: Heinemann, 1996.

Goodman, K. *Phonics Phacts.* Richmond Hill, Ontario: Scholastic Canada Ltd, 1993.

Goodman, K. *What's Whole in Whole Language?* Portsmouth, New Hampshire: Heinemann, 1986.

Halliday, M. *Spoken and Written Language.* 2nd ed. Oxford: Oxford University Press, c1989.

Heath, S. B. *Ways with Words: Language, life, and work in communities and classrooms.* New York: Cambridge University Press, 1983.

Holdaway, D. *The Foundations of Literacy.* Sydney: Ashton Scholastic, 1979.

Holdaway, D. *Independence in Reading.* Auckland: Ashton Educational, 1972.

Holdaway, D. *Stability and Change in Literacy Learning.* Exeter, New Hampshire: Heinemann Educational, 1984.

Kelly, M. and Moore, D. "I've Found My Memory! Reciprocal teaching in a primary school." *SET* 2 (1993).

McNaughton, S. *Patterns of Emergent Literacy: Processes of development and transition.* Melbourne: Oxford University Press, 1995.

Meek, M. *Learning to Read.* London: Bodley Head, 1982.

Mooney, M. *Developing Life-long Readers.* Wellington: Learning Media, 1993.

Mooney, M. *Reading To, With, and By Children.* Katonah, New York: R. C. Owen Publishers, 1990.

Nicholson, T. *Reading and Learning in the Junior Secondary School.* Wellington: Department of Education, 1988.

Palincsar, A. S. and Brown, A. L. "Reciprocal Teaching of Comprehension-fostering and Comprehension-monitoring Activities." *Cognition and Instruction,* vol. 1 (1984), pp. 112–175.

Reading in Junior Classes. Wellington: Learning Media, 1993.

Saxby, M. "The Gift of Wings: The value of literature to children." Saxby, M. and Winch, G. (eds). *Give them Wings: The experience of children's literature.* South Melbourne: Macmillan, 1987.

Smith, F. *Reading Without Nonsense.* New York: Teachers College Press, 1984.

Smith, John W. A. and Elley, W. B. *Learning to Read in New Zealand.* Auckland: Longman Paul, 1994.

Stanovich, K. E. *Differences in Reading Acquisition: Causes and consequences.* Ontario Institute for Studies in Education, paper presented to the Eighteenth Conference on Reading, Wellington, May 1992.

The New Zealand Curriculum Framework. Wellington: Learning Media, 1993.

Tierney, R. J. and Shanahan, T. "Research on the Reading-writing Relationship: Interactions, transactions and outcomes." Barr, R., Kamil, M. L., Mosenthal, P., and Pearson, P. D. (eds). *Handbook of Reading Research 2,* pages 246–80. New York: Longman, 1991.

Tizard, B. and Hughes, M. *Young Children Learning: Talking and thinking at home and at school.* London: Fontana, 1984.

Vygotsky, L. S. *Mind in Society.* Cambridge, Massachusetts: Harvard University Press, 1978.

Wells, G. *The Meaning Makers: Children learning language and using language to learn.* Exeter, New Hampshire: Heinemann Educational, 1986.

Wood, D. *How Children Think and Learn.* New York: Basil Blackwell, 1988.

Index

Acknowledgments

The photographs in this book are by Jamie Lean, except for the following: the photographs on pages 2, 23, 28, 39, 143, and 148; the top photograph on page 11, which is by Barry Clothier; the photograph on page 43, which is by Alan Doak; the photographs on pages 64 and 87, which are by Karen Angus; the top right photo on page 2 and the photographs on pages 72 and 88 which are by S. A'Court; and the photographs from the books *The Praying Mantis* on page 45 and *Snap! Splash!* on page 74, which are by Nic Bishop and are reproduced by permission of Nic Bishop.

The illustration on page 9 from *Can't a Person Have a Friend?* is by Donna Cross.
The illustrations on pages 9 and 109 from *A Name for Rabbit* are by Margaret Clarkson. The text is reproduced by permission of Pat Quinn.
The extracts and illustrations on pages 41, 42, and 60 from the books *Fun with Mo and Toots* and *Where Are My Socks?* are reproduced by permission of Miriam Macdonald.
The extract from *Alice in Wonderland* on page 63 is by Lewis Carroll.
The extract from *The Highwayman* on page 113 is by Alfred Noyes.
The illustration on page 119 from "David Balfour" is by Murray Grimsdale.
The letter from Kaikorai Primary School on page 122 is reproduced by permission of Kaikorai Primary School, Dunedin.
The medley illustration on page 124 is by Amanda Smart.
The page of the article "Make a Water-wheel" (*School Journal,* Part 1 Number 2, 1989) shown on page 130 is reproduced by permission of Brian Birchall.
The icecream recipe on page 130 is by M.K.C. Smith.
The page of civil defence emergency instructions shown on page 130 is reproduced by permission of the New Zealand Ministry of Civil Defence and Telecom Directories Limited.

Thanks to the following for giving permission: Murray Papps of Lever Rexona for the extract on page 10; Dorothy Butler and Richards Literary Agency for the extract on page 11; Routledge for the first extract on page 12; K.E. Stanovich for the extract on page 16; Blackwell Publishers for the extract on page 18; Adobe Systems Inc. for the extract on page 21; Ashton Educational for the extract on page 29; Margaret Mahy for the extract on page 34; The Estate of Olive Harvey for the extract on page 35; Pauline Cartwright for the extract on page 45; Frank Smith Educational Associates for the extract on page 50; Stuart Payne for the extract on page 62; John Hall for the extract on page 78; Heinemann for the extract on page 90; Joy Cowley for the extracts on pages 95 and 127; Macmillan Education Australia for the extracts on page 99; Penguin Books (NZ) Ltd for the extract on page 105; Jack Lasenby for the extract on page 106; David Higham Associates and Jonathan Cape for the second extract on page 107; The New Zealand Council for Educational Research for the extract on page 115; Vivienne Joseph for the poem on page 114; June Walker for the first extract on page 115; David Hill for the second extract on page 115; Reed Consumer Books for the first extract on page 119; Pat Quinn for the extract on page 132; and Transit New Zealand for the artwork on page 132.
The extracts from *Becoming Literate: The construction of inner control* on pages 12, 40 and 79, and *What Did I Write?* on page 29 are reproduced by permission of Marie Clay and Heinemann Education New Zealand. Please note that all of this material is copyright and unauthorised use is liable for prosecution.
All reasonable attempts have been made to locate the copyright holders of the story by Valery Carrick quoted on page 61, and the story by Christiane Moodie quoted on page 107.
Excerpt from BILL MARTIN'S INSTANT READERS, Teacher's Guide, Level 3 by Bill Martin Jr. and Peggy Brogan, copyright © 1972 by Holt, Rinehart and Winston, reprinted by permission of the publisher.

Thanks to the following schools where many of the photographs in this book were taken: Clyde Quay School, Wellington; Mount Cook School, Wellington; Glenfield Intermediate School, Auckland; Paremata School, Paremata; Pencarrow School, Wainuiomata; Plimmerton School, Plimmerton; Rangikura School, Ascot Park; Tawa School, Tawa; and Te Aro School, Wellington.
Thanks also to the students and teachers who provided material for this book.